LIMITS OF
HUMAN PERFORMANCE

American Academy
of Physical Education Papers
No. 18

Fifty-sixth Annual Meeting
Eugene, Oregon
July 19-26, 1984

Published by Human Kinetics Publishers, Inc.
for the American Academy of Physical Education

Editors
David H. Clarke
Helen M. Eckert

Academy Seal designed by
R. Tait McKenzie

ISBN 0-931250-99-4
ISSN 0741-4633

Printed in the United States of America

Copies of this publication may be ordered from:
Human Kinetics Publishers, Inc.
Box 5076, Champaign, IL 61820
(217) 351-5076

CONTENTS

The Scientific Study of Athletes and Athletics

Henry J. Montoye
University of Wisconsin–Madison

The theme for the Academy meetings in this Olympic year, of course, is very appropriate. We are all interested in the application of sport physiology, sport psychology, and sport sociology in raising the level of performance in athletics. And, improvement of records in the Olympic Games during the last few generations has been spectacular. It would be satisfying to conclude that this was all the result of scientific studies of sport. However, we know this is not true. An increase in world population in itself increases the probability that more people will be born with outstanding athletic talent. Some of the improvement in performance may be ascribed to more widespread and efficient recruitment so that now a boy or girl with athletic talent is much more likely to be discovered, and at a younger age. The rising standard of living, particularly in developing countries, must also be responsible for some of the improvement in world records. With a higher standard of living has come more widespread sports participation, and hence athletically talented people are more likely to be identified. Better nutrition and health care has enabled young men and women to come closer to achieving their potential in size and capacity. The shrinking world has made it possible for developing countries to be exposed to other coaching methods and to participate in more world-class competition.

In addition to these major developments, science has certainly played its part in the betterment of Olympic performance. Improvement in equipment, the application of physics to sports, and a greater understanding of the biochemistry and physiology of exercise has brought better training methods. Research in sport psychology has made us more aware of staleness and has increased our understanding of motivation and effective training schedules. Perhaps more important, some of the myths that governed coaching practices in the past have been dispelled.

However, the research which has led to steadily improving athletic performance would hardly be worth the trouble if that were the only effect. Certainly the joy of competition was just as great before the 4-minute mile was a common occurrence. The physical and emotional benefits were likely just as great for the children who practiced the rudimentary gymnastics in the Hassenheide under Friedrich Ludwig Jahn as they are for the boys and girls who perform such fantastic feats on the apparatus today. But research in sports goes beyond the breaking of records. The gifted physiologist, A.V. Hill, was awarded the Nobel prize in medicine in 1922 partly as a result of his research with athletes. However, it was not because his work led to better athletic per-

1

formance that he received this distinction. Rather, it was the clarification of our understanding of physiological mechanisms that ensured him a place in the history of science. The results of his investigations thus apply not only to the athletes he studied, but also to the rest of us who are much less gifted in sports, and even to the sick and handicapped. As stated by another Nobel laureate, Glenn T. Seaborg, "We are interested in the advancement of science because we know that it will result in the advancement of man" (Silverstein, 1979, p. 29).

Contrasting the characteristics of trained athletes with untrained people is a useful research strategy. It is common in science to study extremes in an effort to generate or test hypotheses about mechanisms. This approach has been used many times in studying the effects of exercise. The observation many years ago of the low resting heart rate of endurance athletes was later followed by longitudinal studies in which exercise training was found to lower the resting heart rate and increase the stroke volume of the heart. More recently, differences in muscle fiber types between the endurance athlete and nonathlete have suggested some hypotheses about the effects of regular exercise. When a relationship was suspected between a sedentary life and an increased incidence of coronary heart disease, a host of investigations of endurance athletes were initiated in which such risk factors as blood concentration of cholesterol and other lipids, blood pressure, and cardiac function were measured.

The importance of these investigations rests on the assumption that these subjects are at the upper extreme in physical training and fitness, and that if there is an effect of regular exercise on risk factors, it should manifest itself in the trained athlete. The longevity of outstanding athletes has been studied because it might shed light on the effects of exercise on length of life. Competitive older athletes have been examined to ascertain whether or not exercise influences bone mineralization. Dr. William Busse of the University of Wisconsin Medical School, an asthma specialist, stated, "By studying world-class athletes we are learning a lot about how to help ordinary people. Our goal is to help people lead as full and as active lives as they possibly can " (Wisconsin State Journal, 1984).

There is another practical reason for utilizing athletes in our research. As a group, they are interested in the effects of exercise and how physical performance can be improved. Therefore they are cooperative subjects. Additionally, they are accustomed to exerting maximum effort and to experiencing the pain that such effort may bring; this kind of dedication is essential for conducting some investigations. But perhaps A.V. Hill (1972) came closest to explaining why athletes are so often studied:

> The complaint has been made to me—'why investigate athletics, why not study the processes of industry or of disease?' The answer is twofold. (1) The processes of athletics are simple and measurable and carried out to a constant degree, namely to the utmost of a man's powers: those of industry are not; and (2) athletes themselves, being in a state of health and dynamic equilibrium, can be experimented on without danger and can repeat their performances exactly again and again. I might perhaps state a third reason and say, as I said in Philadelphia, that the study of athletes and athletics is 'amusing': certainly to us and sometimes I hope to them. Which leads to a fourth reason, perhaps the most important of all: that being 'amusing' it may help to bring new and enthusiastic recruits to the study of physiology, which needs every one of them, especially if they be chemists. (Hill, 1927, p. 3)

Thus, I believe everyone present shares my enthusiasm as we anticipate the papers to be presented under the theme that Dr. David Clarke has chosen—The Limits of Human Performance.

REFERENCES

HILL, A.V. (1927). *Muscular movement in man: The factors governing speed and recovery from speed.* New York: McGraw-Hill.

SILVERSTEIN, A. (1979). *Conquest of death.* New York: MacMillan.

WISCONSIN State Journal, (1984, May 13). Section 1, p. 6.

The Limits of Human Performance

David H. Clarke
University of Maryland

Human performance has captured the interest of a wide segment of the population. In addition to the athlete, there is a growing scientific awareness among coaches and researchers. Athletic records are followed by more and more people, and data are meticulously kept by officials of various sports and by the media as well. For an athlete, achieving peak performance is one of the factors that makes competition so self-sustaining.

The growth in size, complexity, and number of research laboratories has provided an impetus for the study of the athletic performer. Data are now available in nearly every sport, and the elite athlete has been described in a variety of scientific journals. Ultimately, it will benefit the performer to have information on which to base future performance and training methods, as well as to help explain the achievement of certain competitive standards.

A question often posed to athletes, trainers, and sport scientists is to what extent existing performance records can be exceeded. To the casual observer, it would seem that we must indeed be reaching the point where further changes are either impossible or improbable. In track events, for example, is it likely that athletes can look forward to exceeding existing world records? Are the limits of human performance being reached in running sports, or are they reaching asymptotic values?

These questions can be answered somewhat by examining the established trends. Knowledge obtained from the progress of past records over time should permit one to speculate on the future changes likely to occur. The limits of performance can probably be most clearly visualized from an examination of the shortest running events. Figure 1 reveals the trend of world record times in the 100 m run and suggests that future times are probably not going to change markedly. An asymptote has nearly been reached in the past 15 years, so further reductions in time will be difficult to achieve.

Beyond that distance, there would appear to be substantial room for improvement. The trend for the 200 m run implies that reductions in time are clearly possible (Figure 2), and this is also true for the 400 and 800 m runs (Figures 3 and 4).

Middle-distance events, such as the mile run and the 1500 m run (Figures 5 and 6), exhibit continuously declining times, although one can observe periods of plateaus, only to be followed by a series of world-record times. This is particularly noticeable in the mile run and is illustrated most dramatically in the so-called breakthrough following a reduction in the record below 4 minutes. The differences in the shapes of the curves for the mile and 1500 m runs are interesting.

4

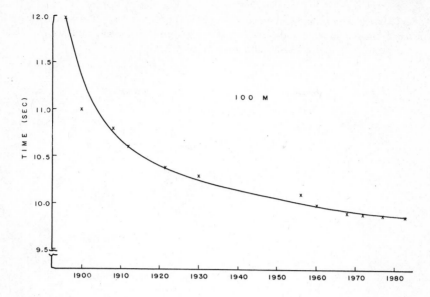

Figure 1— World record performances in the 100 m. run.

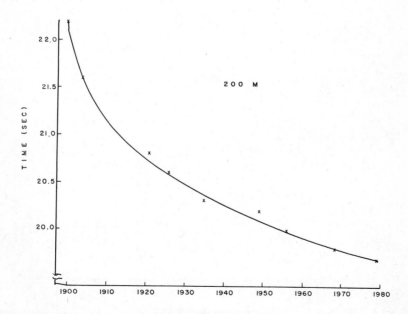

Figure 2— World record performances in the 200 m. run.

The trends for the hurdles seem to follow similar patterns. The 110 m hurdle reveals a very definite asymptotic value in recent years (Figure 7), while there still seems room for improvement in the 400 m hurdles (Figure 8).

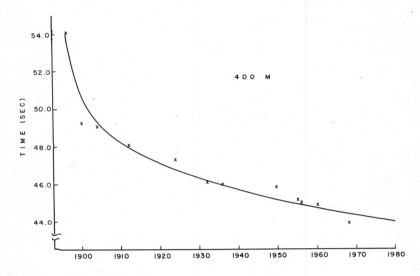

Figure 3— World record performances in the 400 m. run.

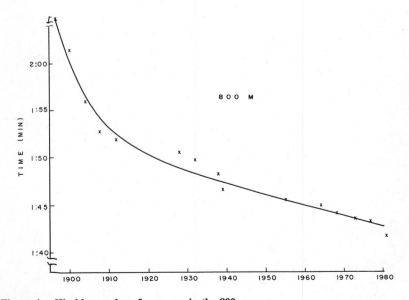

Figure 4— World record performances in the 800 m. run.

Finally, as one would anticipate, the distance events seem to have the greatest room for improvement. It is somewhat difficult to establish a smooth trend for the 5000 m run (Figure 9), but it seems the world record has improved fairly steadily over the

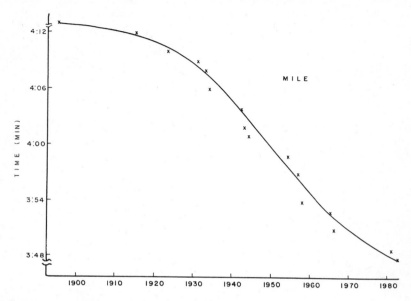

Figure 5— World record performances in the mile run.

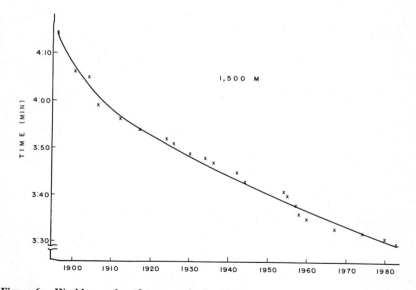

Figure 6— World record performances in the 1500 m. run.

past several years. This appears somewhat less evident for the 10,000 m run (Figure 10), in which recent changes have not been dramatic.

In summary, it seems evident from an analysis of the data for running events that there is ample room for further improvement in performance. One should anticipate that the limits of human performance have not yet been attained. This annual meeting

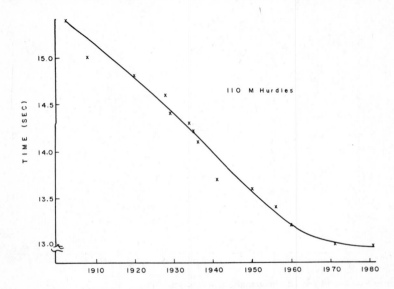

Figure 7— **World record performances in the 110 m. hurdles.**

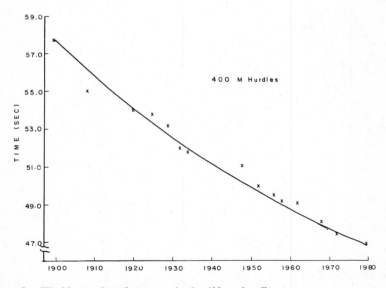

Figure 8— **World record performances in the 400 m. hurdles.**

of the American Academy of Physical Education is dedicated to the theme, "The Limits of Human Performance," and it will be examined from a number of different perspectives during the next series of sessions. From such discourse we may better understand the nature of sport and human activity.

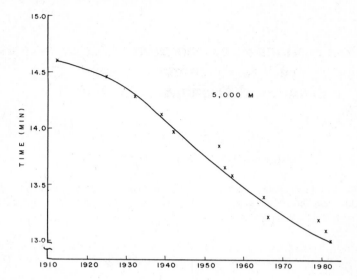

Figure 9— World record performances in the 5000 m. run.

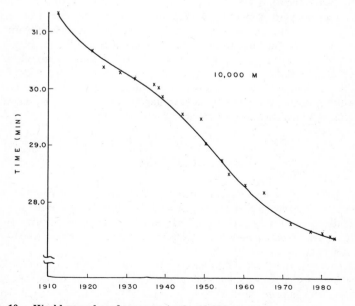

Figure 10— World record performances in the 10,000 m. run.

Observations of Extraordinary Performances in an Extreme Environment and in a Training Environment

E.R. Buskirk
The Pennsylvania State University

The limits of human achievement including endurance continue to be tested in a variety of ways and the results are frequently astonishing. Perhaps former Justice O.V. Holmes portrayed the situation best:

> "Life is action and passion...it is required of a man that he should share the passion and action of his time at the peril of being judged not to have lived." (Holmes in Bartlett, 1980, p.643)

Of the extreme activities that people have engaged in during the past several years, extraordinary feats come to mind such as the swimming double-crossing of the English Channel by a young girl, the setting of a new distance record of something over 600 miles in a 24-hour run, and the grueling performances in triathalons and iron men and women contests. The three feats that I wish to dwell on are the climbing of Mt. Everest without supplementary oxygen, the climbing of the partially sheer East Face of Everest, and the setting of a world weightlifting record by a 16-year old boy. The former feats involve competition in an extreme environment while the latter feat does not. Nevertheless, the weightlifting feat is so impressive that I thought it worthy of emphasis along with extraordinary performances on the highest mountain in the world.

CLIMBING EVEREST

An exceptional event in high terrestrial altitude physiology was the climbing of Mt. Everest in 1978 without supplementary oxygen (Habeler, 1978; Messner, 1979). Although this extraordinary performance has now been repeated a number of times including the solo ascent by Messner in 1980, the feat remains to be classified as truly outstanding in our time.

Sutton, Jones, and Pugh (1983) have reviewed the estimated aerobic capacities of climbers from several mountaineering expeditions and concluded that Habeler and Messner probably have sea level aerobic capacities of 77 to 81 $mlO_2 \cdot kg^{-1} \cdot min^{-1}$, which would yield an aerobic capacity of 10 to 12 $mlO_2 \cdot kg^{-1} \cdot min^{-1}$ at the top of

Mt. Everest. These estimated values are considerably higher (40 to 50%) than those estimated for earlier mountaineers including the climbers involved with the "Silver Hut" expedition by the British (Pugh, 1962). In training, Messner was ostensibly capable of climbing 1,000 m in 34 minutes, representing a power output of approximately 1,800 kpm • min^{-1} or an aerobic capacity of nearly 4 L • min^{-1}.

If it is assumed that climbing at this rate cannot be sustained for any length of time unless it is conducted at a rate that utilizes no more than 80% of $\dot{V}O_2$ max, then Messner's estimated $\dot{V}O_2$ max must be about 5 L • min^{-1} or about 80 ml • kg^{-1} • min^{-1}. This high $\dot{V}O_2$ max was undoubtedly an important variable bearing on the achievement of the Everest summit without supplementary oxygen. Pugh and Sutton (1983) have also assembled estimations of the aerobic capacities of various climbers who participated in several expeditions. Their comparison appears in Table 1. It is clear that Habeler and Messner had superior aerobic capacities that are comparable to those of world-class distance runners. Although the mean $\dot{V}O_2$ max for Habeler and Messner appears somewhat inconsistent with the range cited, the mean is consistent with the estimated value for Messner cited earlier.

Another important factor is that the barometric pressure and, hence, the partial pressure of inspired oxygen (P_IO_2), are both higher at the top of Mt. Everest than predicted from standard equations. Thus, actual P_B exceeds the calculated value by 14 to 17 mmHg, that is, 250 to 253 mmHg actual versus 236 mmHg calculated. Thus P_IO_2 is about 43 mmHg instead of 40 mmHg or slightly below. This additional oxygen is sufficient to enable slightly greater exercise intensity on the mountain, that is, to maintain a $\dot{V}O_2$ of 10 to 12 mlO$_2$ • kg^{-1} • min^{-1}, or roughly 2.5 to 3 times the resting oxygen uptake (Pugh & Sutton, 1983).

Perhaps the best way to describe the struggle to the top and the reactions Habeler and Messner had during the final ascent and their return from the summit is to quote from their writings.

It is that bit of Everest that outstrips the other eight-thousand metre peaks that was the psychological barrier to climbing. Peter Habeler and I dragged ourselves on all fours along the summit ridge in a snowstorm. We could only manage five metre stages before collapsing in the snow, gasping for breath for a full five minutes or more. This was the only way we could compensate for the lack of oxygen and muster sufficient strength to continue. The last 100 metres of height took us more than an hour to climb. (R. Messner, front end paper, 1979)

Table 1

Comparison of Aerobic Capacity Among Climbers

Group	N	VO$_2$ max (mlO$_2$ • kg^{-1} • min^{-1}) Mean	Range
Everest, 1953	5	51	50-54
4 Himalayan expeditions	12	48	41-54
Elite British climbers	4	61	60-65
Habeler & Messner	2	80	71-80

Adapted from Pugh & Sutton, 1983

Rebuffed by a raging storm on their first attempt, the two men draw on their deepest reserves of energy as they crawl to the peak. They succeed, they embrace, they cry. But to spend more than a minute at the top is to assume brain damage. Habeler, his instinct to survive asserting itself, literally tumbles down the mountain coming closest to death immediately after his ultimate triumph. He has not conquered Everest, he says, Everest has merely tolerated him. (P. Habeler, back cover, 1978)

When Peter Habeler and I climbed down from the summit—we were not then fully aware what we had achieved with this mask-free ascent of Everest. In our fatigue there was no sense of success. Added to this we were both suffering—Peter from a damaged Achilles tendon: I with snow-blindness: we both also had light frostbite on our fingers and our noses were peeling. We knew that our push to the topmost point without the aid of oxygen sets, would provoke discussion since most climbers and almost all doctors had prophesized utter failure—today we are greeted with disbelief, for as long at least until we can produce evidence of our climb, or until mask-free ascents become the rule. (R. Messner, 1979, p. 204)

EAST FACE OF EVEREST

The East Face of Everest with an approach through Tibet poses a formidable challenge. It was first reconnoitered by a British team in 1921, but was deemed virtually unclimbable. However, with the development of superior equipment and techniques for rock climbing, the East Face ultimately appeared less formidable. The East Face has a vertical rock face (Lowe Buttress) that extends from 5,425 to 6,492 m (17,800 to 21,300 ft) with another 2,347 m (7,700 ft) to the summit. Following additional reconnaissance in 1980-81, Richard Blum scaled the rock wall but failed to reach the summit. In 1983, J. Morrissey led a 13-member team to the East Face (Harvard & Morrissey, 1984). They took 28 days to complete their staging preparations and 10 days for the final climb. They installed two cargo tramways for translocating climbing gear and supplies. Six climbers ultimately reached the summit following their negotiation of the Lowe Buttress. They carried 30-lb. packs to the staging area above the buttress. Oxygen was utilized only during the final ascent of 914 m (3,000 ft). The threats of avalanches, rock falls, blinding snow, and high winds made the transitions extremely treacherous. Thus, the feat of overcoming the extensive vertical buttress under the extremely hazardous conditions must be characterized as an extraordinary performance.

Climbing Everest with and without supplementary oxygen has exacted a formidable toll over the years. By the end of 1983, some 68 groups representing 21 countries had challenged the peak. At least 62 lives had been lost. Yet, 149 climbers, including four women, have reached the summit and even more are anxious to try. Virtually all routes to the summit have now been successfully attempted. Perhaps climbing the East Face alone without supplementary oxygen remains the final challenge.

CHARACTERISTICS OF BEST FREE CLIMBERS

Several characteristics enable exceptional performance in mountaineering. Those climbers who are extremely able must be physically fit and have a high aerobic capacity. They must also be technically superior climbers who are efficient in their movements on the mountain and who are able to take advantage of the best equipment available.

They undoubtedly have little body fat. They are well acclimatized to hypoxia and have developed considerable tolerance of both hypohydration and semistarvation. They have strong legs and can generate high power-to-body-weight ratios. They must be psychologically stable and capable of withstanding isolation for long periods. They have learned to travel light and have learned the best combinations of climb-to-rest ratios for sustained upward progression. Chances are that they respond to hypoxia by relative hyperventilation and have developed a high cerebral tolerence of hypoxia. They must be somewhat fearless and possess an exceptional sense of body position and balance while transporting moderately heavy loads. Thus, the best free climbers must be exceptional athletes in their own right. Habeler and Messner have these characteristics.

EVEREST SIMULATION

Soon after World War II, a long-term study of acclimation to hypoxia was undertaken in a large hypobaric chamber at the U.S. Navy facility in Pensacola, FL (Houston, 1983; Houston & Riley, 1947). The project was named "Operation Everest," for its purpose was to ascertain whether humans could operate at 8,839 m (29,000 ft) without supplementary oxygen. The acclimation rate was intentionally slow as the four men who served as subjects reached about 6,858 m (22,500 ft) on the 27th day of chamber living. The men were then rested before making a dash to the summit during a 6-hour period. The entire experiment took 35 days to perform.

It is interesting that two of the four men were fit enough and sufficiently well acclimated to pedal a cycle ergometer for 15 to 20 minutes at a simulated barometric pressure of approximately 250 mmHg, equivalent to an altitude of 8,870 m (29,100 ft). The other two men requested oxygen prior to the summit experience. Thus, the strong suggestion was planted that climbers could ascend to the top of Mt. Everest without supplementary oxygen. During the interim between the initial laboratory ascent and the actual feat on the mountain, it was argued that the mountain posed some insurmountable challenges: Not only were the stressors of reduced pressure and fewer oxygen molecules involved, but the environmental conditions on the mountain posed the additional stressors of cold, snow, ice, crevasses, wind, solar radiation, hypohydration, semistarvation, isolation, anxiety, fear, and so forth. Thus, the natural challenge far outstripped the laboratory challenge.

Recently we have seen the development of relatively sophisticated scientific efforts on the mountain (West, 1983) associated with the American medical research expedition to Everest that complement the excellent investigations undertaken in the Silver Hut by Pugh and his colleagues during the 1960-61 British expedition to Everest (Pugh, 1962). Our knowledge should be further extended if the planned "Operation Everest II" is undertaken in the Natick hypobaric chamber this coming fall. A slightly longer period of acclimation to hypoxia is planned (34 days) and the assault on the summit from about 7315 m (24,000 ft) will be more gradual, occupying about 4 days (Sutton, Maher, & Houston, 1983).

A TEENAGE PHENOMENON

The sports medicine community has been cautious in recommending intensive weight training for growing children. Yet in at least one country the cautionary approach has

Table 2

A World Record for the 16-Year-Old Suleimanov at the 1984 World Championships in Vitoria, Spain

Country	Lifter	Snatch (kg)	(lb)	Clean & Jerk (kg)	(lb)	Total (kg)	(lb)
Bulgaria	Suleimanov	130	286	168	370	298	656
USSR	Mirzoyan	(125) (missed 3x)	(275.5)	165.5	364	—	—

Mirzoyan, a former world champion.
Suleimanov's total—A Sinclair formula record of more than three times the lifter's body weight.
Record established by the International Weightlifting Federation.
Adapted from Todd, 1984

been challenged by exposing selected young boys to progressive weight training. The outstanding teenage lifter in Bulgaria who represents the product of Bulgaria's developmental program is a 16-year-old young man named Naim Suleimanov. Naim is 152.4 cm (5 ft) tall and weighs 55.9 kg (124 lb). He was born in 1968 in Ptichar (Thrace), Bulgaria, to parents of Turkish descent who are essentially manual laborers. Naim started lifting at age 9 in an informal way, using a variety of heavy objects. He became an early lifting fan and took the sports school examination after reaching his 11th birthday. He qualified for sports school and entered at age 12. Since then his rise in competitive status has been phenomenal (Todd, 1984).

At age 14, Naim competed in the 52 kg (114 lb) class in Sao Paulo, Brazil. His combined lift total was 250.5 (551 lb). This combined lift total was only 2.5 kg (5.5 lb) under the world record for the open division for the weight class. In Vitoria, Spain, earlier this year, Naim set a world record for the combined lift (snatch plus clean and jerk). He snatched 130 kg (286 lb), cleaned and jerked 168 kg (370 lb), for a total of 298 kg (656 lb). His chief competitor was the former world champion, Mirzoyan, from the Soviet Union, who missed three attempts to snatch 125 kg (275.5 lb) and was therefore ineligible to receive a total lift score. Naim's clean-and-jerk lift set a new Sinclair formula record for the International Weightlifting Federation, for he had lifted more than three times his body weight (Todd, 1984). A summary of this competition appears in Table 2.

The development program that has produced such outstanding results is based on the utilization of sports schools following the screening and selection of outstanding prospects. There are 22 sports schools in Bulgaria that emphasize their premier sport of weightlifting. There are 85 coaches who have weightlifting as their primary responsibility. About 2,000 boys are being coached in weightlifting. The boys receive room and board, athletic clothing, and attend smaller-than-average academic classes. They remain at the school from age 12 to 18 unless they are deemed a mischosen prospect or transfer to the National Training Center as Naim has done. Some observations about the success of the Bulgarian program are as follows:

1. Domination of teenage lifting for about 10 years;
2. Development of many world champions;
3. Achievement of the highest ratio of champions per unit population of any country.

A comparison of the relative emphasis on weightlifting appears in Table 3. The results reveal that the Soviet Union puts greater effort into its program than does Bulgaria. Although the Soviets have achieved considerable success in weightlifting, they have been relatively outstripped by Bulgaria.

The general features of the control of the national as well as the sports schools' training regimens are set forth in Table 4. Although many of the features may help produce champions, it is undoubtedly the high intensity and exceptionally long dura-

Table 3

Comparison of Relative Emphasis on Weightlifting in the USSR and Bulgaria

Country	Registered lifters	Coaches	RL/C
USSR	340,000	2,500	136
Bulgaria	5,000	185	27

Adapted from Todd, 1984

Table 4

General Features of Control of the Training Regimen for Bulgarian Weightlifters

Special diet including:
   yogurt, sheep's milk cheese,
   food supplements
Some fasting
   1 day per 10 or 11 days
Emphasis on staying hungry
Adequate recovery
Adequate sleep
Regular massage
Hydrotherapy
Psychological assessment

Adapted from Todd, 1984

Table 5

Training Session Schedule for Bulgarian
National Team Weightlifters

Monday through Friday
  7 sessions of lifting per day
  10 to 12 sets per session
  @ 90 to 100 + % of previous best
Saturday
  3 sessions of lifting
Sunday
  Day of rest and relaxation
Therefore, intermittant but regular high intensity workouts of appreciable duration

---

Adapted from Todd, 1984

tion of the actual training that is responsible for the outstanding results. Such intense training is carried out perhaps even to a greater extent at the National Training Center—the general features of this top level program are presented in Table 5. This program of regular multisession daily lifting has not usually been followed elsewhere. More frequent days of rest have been traditional.

The question of use of anabolic steroids and other compounds such as growth hormone inevitably comes up in conjunction with such concentrated training programs. According to Todd (1984), K. Glovov, a team physician, has said that steroids are prescribed about twice a year to speed recovery during heavy training, but are used only with athletes who are mature. The emphasis in the Bulgarian program is not on ancillary means to achieve muscle hypertrophy, fiber splitting, and hence greater strength, but on the intensity and duration of training—the primary stimulus.

FIBER SPLITTING

The Bulgarian training regimen involves numerous sets of intense lifting near, at, and frequently surpassing the lifter's previous best. The goal of such intense training is to induce skeletal muscle fiber splitting and thus enhance the strength development process. Although somewhat controversial, this approach is not without its supporters (Gonyea, 1980a).

The conventional thinking, based on years of observation of the behavior of skeletal muscle to physiological overload, is that the cross-sectional area of individual fibers is increased but the number of fibers is not increased. This concept has recently been challenged by Gonyea (1980b), among others, who has observed what has been called fiber splitting in the muscles of cats trained to perform front leg weight lifting. Considering such splitting, the dilemma of what is happening to motor units remains just that—a dilemma—for the motor unit (the organized structural conglomerate responsible for producing movement) consists of an alpha-motoneuron together with the group of fibers that it innervates. Are additional neuronal endings produced to innervate the split fibers or does innervation proceed through the original ending to the attached portion of the fiber and then through elements of this fiber on to the split portion? That is, is there a radial spread of depolarization; and is an asynchrony in this process linked to the splitting (Burke & Edgerton, 1975)?

Gonyea (1980b) has postulated that fast tension development in skeletal muscle, as is essential in successful competitive weightlifting, is conducive to fiber splitting along a longitudinal axis resulting in an increased fiber number. These daughter fibers can also hypertrophy with additional training. Intense, rapid muscular contractions are thought to be essential to the splitting process. Obviously, additional confirmation of this splitting process is needed, particularly in human muscle.

SUMMARY

In any presentation of outstanding achievements, one is always impressed with the exceptional dedication to training inevitably involved in addition to the acquisition of the necessary skill. In each of the feats cited, this training and skill acquisition has been exemplary. Our known physiological limits have been extended and we must try to understand the underlying mechanism modifications that make such feats possible. Hopefully, this understanding will ultimately clarify what these modifications are and how they operate, but it is a rather good bet that the performance frontiers will continue to challenge our knowledge. It is some consolation to note that both with respect to the climbing and lifting achievements, laboratory research paved the way by stimulating the thinking of the adventurous by presenting possibilities and partial rationales.

REFERENCES

BURKE, R.E., & Edgerton, V.R. (1975). Motor unit properties and selective involvement in movement. In J.H. Wilmore (Ed.), *Exercise and sports sciences reviews,* **Vol. 3**. New York: Academic Press.

GONYEA, W.J. (1980a). Role of exercise in inducing increases in skeletal muscle fiber number. *Journal of Applied Physiology. Respiratory, Environmental and Exercise Physiology,* **48**, 421-426.

GONYEA, W.J. (1980b). Muscle fiber splitting in trained and untrained animals. In R.S. Hutton & D.I. Miller (Eds.), *Exercise and sport sciences reviews,* **Vol. 8**, Philadelphia: Franklin Institute Press.

HABELER, P. (1978). *The lonely victory.* New York: Simon & Schuster.

HARVARD, A., & Morrissey, J.D. (1984). The forgotten face of Everest: Conquest of the summit. *National Geographic,* **166**, 71-89.

HOLMES, O.V., Jr. (1980). Memorial Day address. 1884. In J. Bartlett, *Bartlett's familiar quotations.* (E.M. Beck, Ed., 15th ed.) Boston: Little, Brown.

HOUSTON, C.S. (1983). The pressure chamber revisited. A look at the past. In J.R. Sutton, C.S. Houston, & N.L. Jones (Eds.), *Hypoxia, exercise, and altitude: Proceedings of the Third Banff International Hypoxia Symposium.* New York: Alan R. Liss.

HOUSTON, C.S., & Riley, R.L. (1947). Respiratory and circulatory changes during acclimatization to high altitude. *American Journal of Physiology,* **149**, 565-588.

MESSNER, R. (1979). *Everest: Expedition to the ultimate.* New York: Oxford University Press.

PUGH, L.G.C.E. (1962). Physiological and medical aspects of the Himalayan scientific and mountaineering expedition, 1960-61. *British Medical Journal,* **2**, 621-627.

PUGH, L.G.C.E., & Sutton, J.R. (1983). Everest then and now. In J.R. Sutton, C.S. Houston, & N.L. Jones (Eds.), *Hypoxia, exercise and altitude: Proceedings of the Third Banff International Hypoxia Symposium.* New York: Alan R. Liss.

SUTTON, J.R., Jones, N.L., & Pugh, L.G.C.E. (1983). Exercise at altitude. *Annual Review of Physiology,* **45**, 427-437.

SUTTON, J.R., Maher, J.T., & Houston, C.S. (1983). Operation Everest II. In J.R. Sutton, C.S. Houston, & N.L. Jones (Eds.), *Hypoxia, exercise and altitude: Proceedings of the Third Banff International Hypoxia Symposium.* New York: Alan R. Liss.

TODD, T. (1984). Behold Bulgaria's vest-pocket Hercules. *Sports Illustrated,* **60**, 32-46.

WEST, J.B. (1983). American medical expedition to Everest: A study of man during extreme hypoxia. In J.R. Sutton, C.S. Houston, & N.L. Jones (Eds.), *Hypoxia, exercise and altitude: Proceedings of the Third Banff International Hypoxia Symposium.* New York: Alan R. Liss.

Metabolic Requirements of Distance Running

F.J. Nagle and D.R. Bassett, Jr.
University of Wisconsin–Madison

The absolute metabolic stress in a running performance is induced by body size and an interplay of factors including environmental conditions, terrain, speed, distance run, and the running efficiency or economy. The first of these, environmental conditions, is most often limiting when problems of heat dissipation arise. An entire literature has been developed relating to this subject and I won't consider the matter here. I will touch briefly on the influence of wind resistance on metabolism and the influence of terrain, speed, and running economy before focusing on substrate utilization in distance running.

METABOLIC COST OF RUNNING

Data derived from treadmill running experiments in various laboratories indicate that human energy expenditure in level running can be estimated from the following equation (American College of Sports Medicine Guidelines, 1980):

$$\dot{V}O_2 \frac{ml}{Kg \times min^{-1}} = Speed\ (\frac{m}{min}) \times 0.2 \frac{ml0_2}{Kgm} + 3.5 \frac{ml0_2}{Kg \times min^{-1}}$$

The determination represents a steady level of energy expenditure which has been measured over a range of speeds from 150 to 300 meters/min in normal humans. Since in treadmill experiments the running subject is stationary, air resistance is not a factor.

McMiken and Daniels (1976) and our group more recently (Bassett, Giese, Nagle, Ward, Raab, & Balke, 1984) have shown that at distance running speeds, the energy expenditure overground on level terrain does not differ from that measured on the treadmill (Figure 1). Air resistance did not exert a measurable influence.

Pugh (1970) published data to show that $\dot{V}O_2$ in running overground increases exponentially with the velocity of the run:

$$\Delta\dot{V}O_2 = .002\ Velocity^3$$

where velocity is measured in meters/sec. The magnitude of the change in $\dot{V}O_2$ due to air resistance over distance running speeds is shown in Figure 2. The effect of air

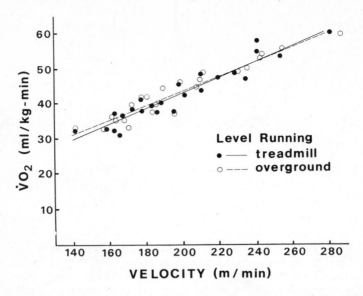

Figure 1—Energy expenditure ($\dot{V}O_2$) in level running at various speeds on treadmill. n = 7

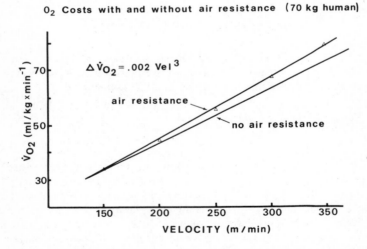

Figure 2—Energy expenditure ($\dot{V}O_2$) in level running at different speeds on treadmill (no air resistance) and overground breaking air (air resistance).

resistance is negligible at 150 meters/min and it increases to about 5.7 ml O_2/Kg × min^{-1} at 350 meters/min speed. One must remember that this is an effect of breaking still air. Any headwind would contribute an addition to this cost.

ECONOMY OF RUNNING

Conley and Krahenbuhl (1980), Daniels, Scardina, and Foley (1984), and Bransford and Howley (1977) have shown that trained runners perform more economically (lower energy expenditure at a given running speed) than nontrained runners. From data of Conley and Krahenbuhl (1980) (Figure 3), it is clear that the energy expenditure may be 15% less on the average over a range of running speeds for elite runners ($\dot{V}O_2$ max 71.7 ml O_2/Kg $\times$ min $-$ 1). It is also interesting to note in the same study that even among elite performers the variability in energy expenditure at various running speeds was 17%, a result confirmed by Daniels et al. (1984).

Recently, Daniels et al. investigated whether economy of running effort carried over to other exercise modes, namely cycling, stepping, walking, and arm cranking in trained runners ($\dot{V}O_2$ max = 67.9 ml/Kg $\times$ min $-$ 1). Table 1 shows their results, which indicate that despite wide differences in running economy in the five most economical compared to the five least economical, it did not carry over to other exercise modes. I would also point out that predicted $\dot{V}O_2$ from the American College of Sports Medicine (ACSM) equation for the running speeds shown in Table 1 are 49.5, 53.0, and 57.1 ml/Kg $\times$ min $-$ 1, respectively, values exceeding the costs for the least economical trained runners. Daniels et al. (1984) speculate that greater economy in energy expenditure can only partly be accounted for by changes in skill through practice, and that greater efficiency is at least partly determined by genetic factors. Improvements in the economy of effort which do result from practice appear to apply equally to all individuals, producing as much variability in $\dot{V}O_2$ submaximal running speeds as is seen in performing less familiar tasks.

Conley and Krahenbuhl (1980) have shown that with elite runners the greater economy in energy expenditure in 10,000-meter races can explain 65.4% of the varia-

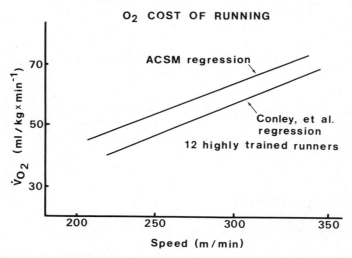

Figure 3—Energy expenditure ($\dot{V}O_2$) in level running at different speeds. Top regression line prediction equation American College of Sports Medicine. Bottom regression line represents energy demands at various speeds for 12 highly trained runners.

Table 1

Comparisons of Energy Expenditures for Various Exercise Modes in Trained Runners

	Most economical $N = 5$	Least economical $N = 5$	Significance
$\dot{V}O_2$ max (ml/kg × min^{-1})	66.9 ± 7.1	68.1 ± 2.2	NS
Arms (ml/min)	1272 ± 85	1282 ± 84	NS
Step (ml/kg × min^{-1})	38.8 ± 3.3	39.0 ± 2.1	NS
Cycle 600 KPM (ml/min)	1525 ± 58	1546 ± 87	NS
Cycle 900 KPM	2034 ± 81	2129 ± 51	NS
Cycle 1200 KPM	2679 ± 22	2785 ± 76	$p < .05$
Walk 15% (ml/kg × min^{-1})	41.2 ± 1.7	41.8 ± 2.1	NS
Walk 17.5%	46.6 ± 2.2	46.9 ± 1.7	NS
Walk 20%	52.0 ± 1.9	51.8 ± 2.6	NS
Run 230 m/min (ml/kg × min^{-1})	41.3 ± 0.6	45.8 ± 2.4	$p < .02$
Run 248 m/min	45.2 ± 1.2	50.5 ± 2.2	$p < .01$
Run 268 m/min	50.3 ± 0.8	55.1 ± 2.3	$p < .01$

Modified from Daniels et al., 1984

tion observed in race performances. This confirmed previous observations of Costill, Thomason, and Roberts (1973), which indicated that the percent $\dot{V}O_2$ max running at a speed of 268 meters/min correlated highly ($r = -.94$) with 10,000-meter race times.

GRADE RUNNING OVERGROUND AND ENERGY EXPENDITURE

Guidelines for exercise testing from ACSM state that the O_2 cost for the vertical component in treadmill grade running is one-half that for overground running. The vertical component cost added to that for level treadmill running is:

$$\dot{V}O_2(\frac{m1O_2}{Kg \times min^{-1}}) = Speed\ (\frac{m}{min})\ (\%\ grade\ \times\ 1.8\ \frac{m1O_2}{Kgm})\ (0.5)$$

and that for overground grade running is

$$\dot{V}O_2(\frac{m1O_2}{Kg \times min^{-1}}) = Speed\ (\frac{m}{min})\ (\%\ grade\ \times\ 1.8\ \frac{m1O_2}{Kgm})$$

Recently Bassett et al. (1984) compared energy costs in running on a 5.7% grade on a treadmill and overground. They found no difference in costs. So, whether or not man moves with reference to a stationary surface or the surface moves with reference to stationary man, it has no relevance to energy expenditure. The data do raise a question regarding the applicability of the constant $1.8 \times m10_2/Kgm$ in estimating energy cost of doing mechanical work. The constant applies reasonably well in walking on a grade, cycling, and stepping vertically. We are not sure why it does not apply in running, but we are pursuing the notion that the inefficient energy expenditure in vertically displacing the center of gravity in level running at least partially converts to useful energy expenditure in grade running. The bottom line is that overground hill running can be predicted from treadmill grade running with corrections only for air and wind resistance.

PROTEIN, FAT AND CHO UTILIZATION

The past 10 years have been marked by a resurgence of interest in the study of protein utilization in exercise. The classical view held that in strenuous, acute exercise of even 2 to 3 hours duration, protein contributed as little as 2% of the energy calories. This figure was based on urea nitrogen concentrations in urine. More recent studies by Lemon, Dolny, and Sherman (1982), on men and women performing in the 26-Km run, found that protein contributed 6% of the energy calories when blood, urine, and sweat urea N was measured. The same investigators (1982) and others (Lemon & Mullin, 1980; Refsum, Gjessing, & Strömme, 1979), showed that in glycogen depleted subjects exercising for 1 hour, or in very prolonged exercise (70 to 90 Km ski races, inducing the equivalent of a starvation state), the protein contribution to total calories provided as much as 10 to 18% of the total.

With the nutritional state maintained by distance runners today, there is no evidence that runs of even marathon distance are associated with anything approaching a starvation state. Hartung, Myhre, Nunneley, and Tucker (1984) recently published data to show that at the end of marathon runs, exogenous glucose was normal and FFA was four times the rest level (Table 2).

Clearly fat and CHO remain the principal sources of energy substrate in endurance performances. Essen's (1977) data (Table 3) show that skeletal muscle contains stores of glycogen and triglycerides for direct use as energy substrate. Glycogen appears to be equally concentrated in Type I and Type II fibers, while triglycerides have three times the concentration in Type I as compared to Type II fibers. It can also be shown that adipose tissue stores in excess of 100,000 kilocalories of energy in tryglycerides and a store of 400 kilocalories of glucose is available from liver.

Glucose derived from muscle glycogen appears to be the ''starter'' substrate at the onset of exercise. This is confirmed from RQ observations (Christensen & Hansen, 1939) and clinical data from McArdle's syndrome patients (Newsholme & Start, 1981), who experience great difficulty with sudden onset of exercise since they lack the glycogen degrading enzyme phosphorylase. Endogenous and exogenous glycerides also contribute early to the substrate pool since serum levels of FFA are decreased over the first 5 minutes of acute exercise as exogenous glycerides are slowly mobilized from adipose tissue.

The use of substrate appears to be regulated ultimately by the ATP/ADP ratio (Holloszy, Rennie, Hickson, Conlee, & Hagberg, 1977; Newsholme & Start, 1981), governing the activity of key enzymes in intermediary metabolism. This regulation is

Table 2

Energy Substrate Changes During Marathon Running in Male and Female Groups*

	M (n = 6)		F (n = 5)	
Time (h)	3.57 ±	0.2	4.17 ±	0.2
Wt lost (%)	3.2 ±	1.4	2.9 ±	0.9
Glucose (mg·dl⁻¹)				
Control	115.2 ±	11	105.8 ±	4.0
Finish	114.1 ±	16	109.6 ±	16
FFA (μ g·1⁻¹·10⁻¹)				
Control	7.36 ±	0.9	6.42 ±	1.3
Finish	31.56 ±	3.4**	28.40 ±	3.2**
U/S FFA				
Control	1.59 ±	0.2	1.53 ±	0.2
Finish	3.28 ±	0.2**	3.63 ±	0.2**

*Values are means ± S.E.
**$p < 0.01$ control-finish
Hartung et al., 1984

Table 3

Triglyceride and Glycogen Concentration in Type I and II Fibers in Humans (dissected out from freeze-dried biopsies)*

	Type I	Type II
Triglyceride mmole/kg dry weight	207 ± 86	74 ± 46
Glycogen mmole/kg dry weight	355 ± 140	359 ± 92

*Values are means ± standard deviations of 17 subjects and are taken from Essen, 1977.

such that even at marathon distances in a normal- to carbohydrate-loaded state, active muscle is presented continuously with normal extracellular glucose levels and FFA levels far exceeding rest (Hartung et al., 1984).

The aerobic nature of the exercise at marathon intensities, and the availability of circulating FFA passively taken up by active muscle cells in proportion to serum concentration, assures elevated FFA oxidation in maintaining a steady exercise state ATP/ADP ratio. The production of citrate in the Krebs Cycle as a result of FFA ox-

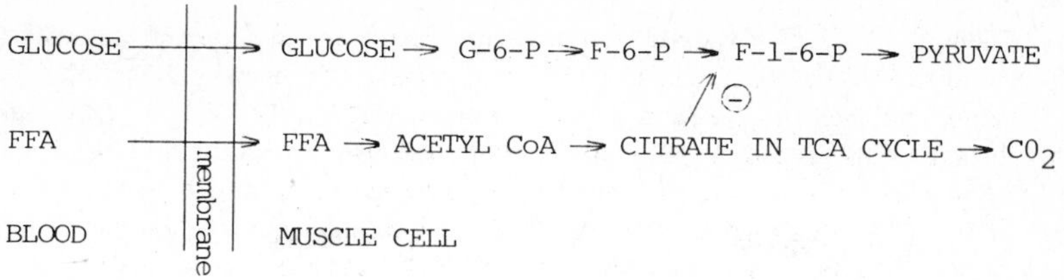

GLUCOSE
GLUCOSE → G-6-P → F-6-P → F-1-6-P → PYRUVATE
FFA
FFA → ACETYL CoA → CITRATE IN TCA CYCLE → CO_2
BLOOD
membrane
MUSCLE CELL

Figure 4—Illustration showing production of citrate in metabolizing FFA. Citrate in turn inhibits phosphofructokinase, the enzyme catalyzing reaction of Fructose-6-phosphate to Fructose-1-6-phosphate.

REGULATION IN METABOLISM
Glucose
Glucose
G-6-P
F-6-P
FDP
MUSCLE CELL
BLOOD
AMP
ATP
ADP
Pyruvate
CO_2 + H_2O
TCA cycle and electron transport chain
acetyl-CoA
Pyruvate
MITOCHONDRION

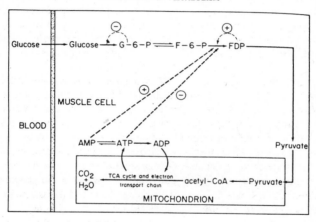

Figure 5—Illustration of AMP activation of phosphofructokinase as a decreased ATP/ADP ratio produced AMP and NH_4^+ another activator of phosphofructokinase. (Newsholme, 1981)

idation inhibits the enzyme phosphofructokinase in the glycolytic pathway, reducing glucose utilization (Figure 4). If this exercise homeostasis is upset by increased exercise intensity, a decrease in the ATP/ADP ratio will again occur, supplying more ADP, AMP, and NH^+, all activators of phosphofructokinase, the rate-limiting enzyme in glycolysis (Figure 5).

Aerobic training has been shown to cause a doubling of mitochondrial density in muscle (Holloszy et al., 1977), accounting for a greater aerobic capacity of the muscle cell and less demand for ATP per mitochondrion at a given submaximal work rate. The reduced imbalance in the ATP/ADP ratio and greater aerobic capacity of muscle with training make possible greater fat oxidation in distance running and a conservation of carbohydrate energy reserves. The ''turning on'' of glycolytic activity to produce ATP aerobically and/or anaerobically now occurs at a higher intensity of running.

The point at which glycolytic activity is greatly accelerated in exercise is marked by continually increased lactic acid (LA) levels in intracellular and extracellular fluid, LA being a product of glycolysis with anaerobic synthesis of ATP. It is quite clear that distance runs exceeding 10,000 meters are performed at 60 to 90% of the maximal O_2 uptake ($\dot{V}O_2$ max). These limits prevail in the human because of the physiological influence of LA which would accumulate at run intensities demanding energy in excess of 60% $\dot{V}O_2$ max in untrained, and 80-90% $\dot{V}O_2$ in the trained. Aside from inducing an acidic state in body fluids, the added H^+, due to LA dissociation, stimulates ventilation for acid-base compensatory purposes. Furthermore, the H^+ is associated with muscle fatigue. Sustained run performances, then, occur at speeds demanding energy just below the level at which glycolysis is accelerated to the point where LA continually increases in body fluids.

As recently as the late 1960s, a series of papers from Margaria's laboratory in Milan (Margaria, Cerretelli, DiPrampero, Massari, & Torrelli, 1963; Saiki, Margaria, & Cuttica, 1967) purported to show that LA production was minimal up to exercise intensities of 90 to 100% $\dot{V}O_2$ max. They also stated that the LA produced at these levels resulted from glycolytic activity occurring at the onset of exercise when the ATP/ADP ratio is suddenly reduced with the effect of inducing glycolysis and LA production. Once the aerobic requirement was met at less than 100% $\dot{V}O_2$, LA was not produced.

In 1970, papers appeared from our own (Nagle, Robinhold, Howley, Daniels, Baptista, & Stoedefalke, 1970) and Costill's laboratory (Costill, 1970) refuting this thesis. Our work (Figure 7) showed that when subjects ran on a treadmill at a mean of 86% $\dot{V}O_2$ max, LA in blood increased over the duration of the exercise and pH decreased accordingly. The data indicate that for these subjects ($\dot{V}O_2$ max 52.9 ml/kg $\times$ min $-$ 1) an energy demand approximating 86% $\dot{V}O_2$ max was associated with a lactate threshold. This is defined here as the point above which serum lactate continually increases and where adequate physiological compensation cannot be made as a run continues. At run demands at or below 77% $\dot{V}O_2$ max, some compensation occurs as evidenced by the leveling of LA in blood and an alkaline pH of body fluids (Figure 6).

An abundant literature has developed around the concept of the lactate threshold. Various groups have reported that a 1 mMolar, 2.5 mMolar, and 4.0 mMolar increase

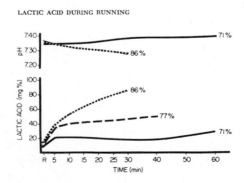

LACTIC ACID DURING RUNNING

Figure 6—Mean LA values (mg%) and pH values over duration of constant speed runs at 82-89%, 74-79%, and 67-74% $\dot{V}O_2$ max.

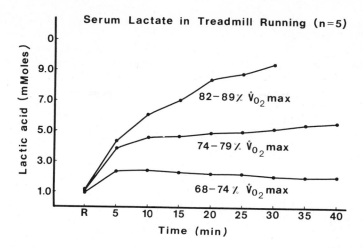

Figure 7—Lactate (mmoles) at 82-89%, 74-79%, and 67-74% $\dot{V}O_2$ max over 30- to 40-minute runs.

in blood lactate in exercise marks the onset of the lactate threshold. While such a criterion may have predictive value in assessing endurance performance as many have suggested (LaFontaine, Londeree, & Spath, 1981; Farrell, Wilmore, Coyle, Billing, & Costill, 1979; Wasserman, 1984), it does not necessarily mark the point of a continuous increase in measured LA in exercise. Our data (Figure 7) show that even a 4 mMolar mean increase in lactate early in running exercise at 74 to 78% $\dot{V}O_2$ max does not signal a continuous rise in blood lactate. This response could reflect only an early anaerobiosis and decreased uptake of lactate by liver and kidney, organs to which blood flow is diminished. It could also reflect a balance between continued LA production and uptake during exercise, which is more likely. Only in running at intensities between 82 to 89% $\dot{V}O_2$ max is blood lactate clearly rising over the duration of the runs, signaling that production is exceeding uptake.

   This particular discussion relates to the question of why muscle and body fluid lactate rises at all in exercise performed within one's maximal aerobic capacity. Costill et al. (1973) invoked the size principal of motor unit recruitment. At more intense running speeds with energy demands approaching aerobic limits, more fast twitch glycolytic motor units, specialized to produce ATP anaerobically, are recruited with production of LA. Recently Saltin and Gollnick (1983) took exception to this view, citing the fact that although LA may increase at 60 to 70% $\dot{V}O_2$ max, the LA concentration may wane with exercise time. They make the point that such a pattern of LA disappearance is not consistent with progressive recruitment of fast twitch glycolytic motor units. I would suggest that the observation of Saltin and Gollnick (1983) detracts little from Costill's thesis. The fact is, as the energy requirement exceeds 60 to 70% $\dot{V}O_2$ max, the exercise is marked by increased LA (Figure 8). The level of LA in blood with time, at a given percent of $\dot{V}O_2$ max, represents only a balance between LA production and muscle and liver uptake of LA. It does not necessarily mean that LA production is reduced. By the time work intensity demands approximately 80% $\dot{V}O_2$ max, it is clear that LA production continuously exceeds uptake as additional fast twitch, highly glycolytic motor units are recruited.

Our data suggest that levels of LA up to 4mMolar in concentration can be tolerated in distance runs. LA values as high as 3.0 and 3.8mMoles have been observed following marathon runs (Costill & Fox, 1969; Farrell et al., 1979). A 4mMolar concentration of LA in blood appears reasonable as a marker of a lactate threshold, the point above which lactate production continuously increases in an exercise effort.

SUMMARY

I have made the case that metabolic costs do not differ at distance running speeds overground or on the treadmill, level or at grade, except for small differences due to air resistance. It is also true that distance running energy requirements may vary widely (as much as 15 to 20%). Some of the economy in running is attributed to training but genetic endowment is an important factor.

Given a normal- to a carbohydrate-loaded state, there is no evidence to indicate that runs up to a marathon distance are marked by any appreciable use of protein as energy substrate. At marathon distances, runs are marked by fat and carbohydrate use, regulated by ATP/ADP ratio, availability of fat, and activity of phosphofructokinase, the key enzyme in glycolysis.

At distance run intensities, speeds are governed metabolically by a lactate threshold. The speed selected is just under the point at which glycolytic production of LA increases continuously with time. A LA production of 4 mMolar represents a minimal LA production level, marking increased and predominating use of carbohydrate for energy calories. LA production at exercise intensities requiring less than 100% of aerobic power is probably attributable to recruitment of FT motor units more specialized for synthesis of ATP through glycolysis with LA as the end product.

REFERENCES

AMERICAN College of Sports Medicine. (1980). *Guidelines for graded exercise testing and exercise prescription* (2nd ed.). Philadelphia: Lea & Febiger.

BASSETT, D.R., Giese, M.D., Nagle, F.J., Ward, A., Raab, D.M., & Balke, B. (1984). Aerobic requirements of overground versus treadmill running. *Medicine and Science in Sports*. Submitted for publication.

BRANSFORD, D.R., & Howley, E.J. (1977). Oxygen cost of running in trained and untrained men and women. *Medicine and Science in Sports*, **9**, 41-44.

CHRISTENSEN, E.H., & Hansen, O. (1939). Arbeitsfähigkeit und ehrinährung. *Scandinavian Archives Physiology*, **81**, 160.

CONLEY, D.L., & Krahenbuhl, G.S. (1980). Running economy and distance running performance of highly trained athletes. *Medicine and Science in Sports*, **12**, 357-360.

COSTILL, D.L. (1970). Metabolic responses during distance running. *Journal of Applied Physiology*, **28**, 251-255.

COSTILL, D.L. & Fox, E.L. (1969). Energetics of marathon running. *Medicine and Science in Sports*, **1**, 81-86.

COSTILL, D.L., Thomason, H., & Roberts, E. (1973). Fractional utilization of the aerobic capacity during distance running. *Medicine and Science in Sports*, **5**, 248-252.

DANIELS, J.T., Scardina, N.J., & Foley, P. (1984). $\dot{V}O_2$ Submax during five modes of exercise. In N. Bachl, L. Prokop, & R. Suckert (Eds.), *Current topics in sports medicine*. Baltimore: Urban & Schwarzenberg.

ESSEN, B. (1977). Intramuscular substrate utilization during prolonged exercise: In P. Milvy (Ed.), *Marathon: Physiological, medical, epidemiological and psychological studies*. New York: New York Academy of Sciences.

FARRELL, P.A., Wilmore, J.H., Coyle, E.F., Billing, J.E., & Costill, D.L. (1979). Plasma lactate accumulation and distance running performance. *Medicine and Science in Sports*, **11**, 338-344.

HARTUNG, G.H., Myhre, L.G., Nunneley, S.A., & Tucker, D.M. (1984). Plasma substrate response in men and women during marathon running. *Aviation, Space and Environmental Medicine*, **55**, 128-131.

HOLLOSZY, J.O., Rennie, M.J., Hickson, R.C., Conlee, R.K., & Hagberg, J.M. (1977). Physiological consequences of the biochemical adaptations to endurance exercise. In P. Milvy (Ed.), *The Marathon: Physiological, medical, epidemiological and psychological studies*. New York: New York Academy of Sciences.

LAFONTAINE, T.P., Londeree, B.R., & Spath, W.K. (1981). The maximal steady state versus selected running events. *Medicine and Science in Sports and Exercise*, **13**, 190-192.

LEMON, P.W.R., Dolny, D.G., & Sherman, B.A. (1982). Effect of prolonged running on protein catabolism. In H.G. Knuttgen, J.A. Vogel, & J. Poortsmans (Eds.), *Biochemistry of Exercise*, Vol. 13. Champaign, IL: Human Kinetics.

LEMON, P.W.R., & Mullin, J.P. (1980). Effect of initial glycogen levels on protein catabolism during exercise. *Journal of Applied Physiology*, **48**, 624-629.

MARGARIA, R., Cerretelli, P., DiPrampero, E., Massari, C., & Torrelli, G. (1963). Kinetics and mechanism of oxygen debt contraction in man. *Journal of Applied Physiology*, **18**, 371-377.

MCMIKEN, D.F., & Daniels, J.T. (1976). Aerobic requirements and maximal aerobic power in treadmill and track running. *Medicine and Science in Sports*, **8**, 14-17.

NAGLE, F.J., Robinhold, D., Howley, E., Daniels, J.T., Baptista, G., & Stoedefalke, K. (1970). Lactic acid accumulation during running at submaximal aerobic demands. *Medicine and Science in Sports*, **2**, 182-186.

NEWSHOLME, E.A., & Start, C. (1981). *Regulation in metabolism*. New York: Wiley.

PUGH, L.B.C.E. (1970). Oxygen intake in track and treadmill running with observations on the effect of air resistance. *Journal of Physiology*, **207**, 823-835.

REFSUM, H.E., Gjessing, R., & Strömme, S.B. (1979). Changes in plasma amino acid distribution and urine amino acid excretion during prolonged heavy exercise. *Scandinavian Journal Clinical Laboratory Investigation*, **39**, 407-413.

SAIKI, H.R., Margaria, R., & Cuttica, F. (1967). Lactic acid production in submaximal work. *Internationale Zeitschrift für Angewandte Physiologie einschliesslich Arbeitsphysiologie*, **24**, 57-61.

SALTIN, B., & Gollnick, P.D. (1983). Skeletal muscle adaptability: Significance for metabolism and performance. In L.D. Peachey (Ed.), *Skeletal muscle*. Bethesda, MD: American Physiology Society.

WASSERMAN, K. (1984). The anaerobic threshold measurement to evaluate exercise performance. *American Review Respiratory Diseases*, **129**, Suppl., 35-40.

Aspects of Anaerobic Performance

James S. Skinner and Don W. Morgan
Arizona State University

Although factors associated with performance of aerobic activities have been studied extensively, less attention has been devoted to factors contributing to anaerobic performance. The primary reason for this is that aerobic activities are much easier to study; that is, once a steady state in oxygen consumption is reached, measurements can be easily obtained and they vary little from minute to minute or from day to day. Similarly, if there is a plateau in oxygen intake during maximal exercise ($\dot{V}O_2$ max), this is an objective, stable measure. On the other hand, anaerobic exercise is much more difficult to measure, as there are no universally accepted criteria or standards, no steady state is achieved and performance is subjective in that it depends on the willingness of people to push themselves. Furthermore, there are various categories of anaerobic performance; these are sometimes put together into only one category, unnecessarily complicating an already complex aspect of performance.

Therefore, this paper will propose a modification of the usual manner in which activities are classified. Using this new system, it will then present and discuss the various protocols for testing anaerobic performance and the effects of various training programs on anaerobic performance.

CLASSIFICATION OF ACTIVITY

Present Classifications

Activity can be classified broadly by the type being performed. For example, prolonged, low-intensity, dynamic, and continuous activities stressing endurance tend to be aerobic (with oxygen), while brief, high-intensity, static, and intermittent activities emphasizing speed and strength tend to be anaerobic (without oxygen). Depending on the activity, however, some characteristics can be applied to both categories (e.g., golf can be brief and intermittent but the intensity may be so low that it is predominantly aerobic). Thus, this classification is too imprecise.

Activity also can be classified by the predominant source of energy being used. Fox, Robinson, and Wiegman (1969) classified activities as follows: (a) <30 sec, ATP-CP; (b) 30-90 sec, ATP-CP and lactate; (c) 90-180 sec, lactate and oxygen; and (d)

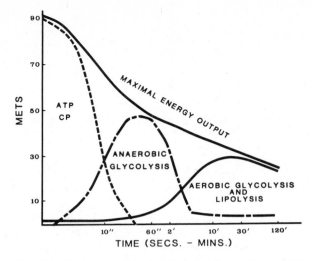

Figure 1—Maximal energy output possible and the relative contribution of various energy-producing systems over time.

>180 sec, oxygen. As will be discussed, however, this system does not adequately describe the energy sources at the various durations.

Figure 1 depicts the maximal energy output possible over time and the relative contribution of the continuously changing energy sources. Because phosphagens (ATP and CP) are stored in the muscle and can be rapidly degraded, they represent the immediate energy source for exercise that is brief (1 to 10 sec) and intense (80-90 times the resting metabolism, or 300%-375% $\dot{V}O_2$ max). The energy for high-intensity exercise (45-50 times resting energy levels, or 200%-225% $\dot{V}O_2$ max) lasting 20-45 sec is primarily supplied by anaerobic glycolysis, with its associated production of lactic acid (LA). With increasing duration, maximal power output drops as energy is supplied more and more by the slower aerobic processes. Aerobic metabolism is the major source of energy after 10 min of continuous exercise. This classification system is also inadequate in that it does not categorize those high-intensity activities lasting 1 to 8 min that are both aerobic and anaerobic.

Proposed Classification

What do we know about these activities and how they should be classified? Figure 2 demonstrates the well-known relationship between intensity and duration of exercise. If intensity is low, duration can be long and the activity is predominantly aerobic. Conversely, if intensity is high, duration must be brief and the activity is primarily anaerobic. The rapidly rising portion of the curve in Figure 2 is generally associated with intensities of 95% to 200% $\dot{V}O_2$ max. The supply of energy at these intensities is both aerobic and anaerobic, and the exercise can usually be performed for 1 to 8 min.

Interestingly, LA levels at the end of 1 to 8 min of maximal exercise tend to be similar. Using data from one subject, Osnes & Hermansen (1972) showed that blood

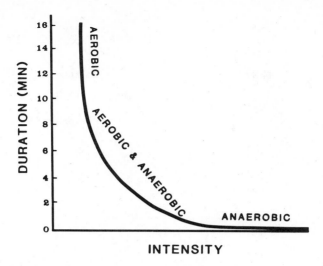

Figure 2—Relation between intensity and duration of exercise and the corresponding energy source.

LA concentrations of about 20 mM were reached after 1 min of treadmill running, while values of 17-18 mM were found after 2 to 8 min. Kindermann & Keul (1977) reported the highest group LA values after 60-75 sec and slightly lower levels after 2 to 8 min of running, swimming, or speed skating. Also, Karlsson (1971) found similar muscle LA levels after 2 to 7 min of maximal exercise. At durations longer than 10 min, muscle and blood LA concentrations from all three studies tended to be lower as intensity decreased and the aerobic system became the major source of energy. Figure 3 combines the data from Osnes & Hermansen (1972) and Kindermann & Keul (1977).

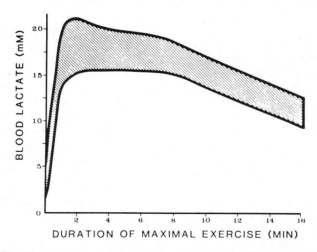

Figure 3—Blood lactic acid levels at various durations of maximal exercise (based on data from Osnes & Hermansen, 1972 and Kindermann & Keul, 1977).

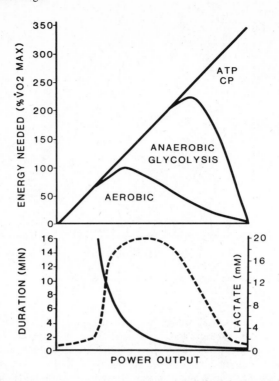

Figure 4—Schematic representation. Top: Energy needed to perform various power outputs, expressed as a percentage of the maximal aerobic power ($\dot{V}O_2$ max), and the relative contribution of aerobic metabolism, anaerobic glycolysis, and phosphagens (ATP & CP). Bottom: Duration of exercise possible and blood lactate at the various power outputs.

These data suggest that a limiting factor in the performance of high-intensity activity lasting 1 to 8 min is the ability to tolerate high concentrations of LA (Gollnick & Hermansen, 1973; Mader, Liesen, Heck, Philippi, Rost, Schürch, & Hollmann, 1976).

Figure 4 is a schematic attempt to combine information from various sources and to provide a basis for the proposed system of classification. At the top of the figure, the diagonal line shows the concept that a given amount of power output requires a given amount of energy (i.e., ATP), regardless of the source. Energy required is presented here relative to the $\dot{V}O_2$ max of an average individual. The areas below the diagonal represent an estimate of the relative contribution of phosphagens, anaerobic glycolysis, and aerobic metabolism at each power output. The lower half of Figure 4 shows the corresponding exercise durations and blood LA concentrations.

Starting at the lowest power output (i.e., rest), blood LA concentration is about 1 mM and energy is supplied by the aerobic system. At 40%-50% $\dot{V}O_2$ max, LA rises to around 2 mM (Skinner & McLellan, 1980), energy is supplied aerobically, and the average person can work for 8 hours a day (Åstrand, 1960). Around 65%-75% $\dot{V}O_2$ max, LA is increased to about 4 mM, anaerobic glycolysis begins to supply a small portion of the energy (Skinner & McLellan, 1980), and exercise can be performed for more than an hour (Costill, 1970; Kindermann, Simon, & Keul, 1978; Saltin, 1971). The anaerobic system becomes increasingly involved in the production of energy as one approaches the maximal aerobic power ($\dot{V}O_2$ max). As a result, LA increases markedly at intensities greater than 75% $\dot{V}O_2$ max, reaching 14-15 mM at an intensity of 95% $\dot{V}O_2$ max and about 18 mM at 100% $\dot{V}O_2$ max. Exercise duration drops rapidly during this rise in intensity and the average person can exercise for only 4 to 6 min at 100% $\dot{V}O_2$ max.

The fact that LA levels stay elevated for up to 8 min suggests that anaerobic glycolysis is a major contributor of energy for longer than the 3 min in the classification of Fox et al. (1969). From about 95% to 200% $\dot{V}O_2$ max, anaerobic glycolysis provides more and more energy, LA accumulates more rapidly until maximal tolerable levels are attained and exercise duration decreases from 8 min to 1 min. Gollnick & Hermansen (1973) estimate that 60% of the energy for maximal exercise lasting 1 min comes from anaerobic glycolysis.

As the exercise duration falls below 1 min, there is less and less time to accumulate LA, even though the rate of anaerobic glycolysis is very high. It has been estimated that approximately 80% of the total energy needed for a 30-sec, all-out bicycle ergometer ride comes from anaerobic glycolysis (Bar-Or, 1981), while the remainder includes small contributions from the aerobic and phosphagen systems. Bar-Or (1981) classified the maximal power output in 30 sec as the "anaerobic capacity."

With increasing power output, the phosphagens are used more, while the aerobic and anaerobic systems are used less. Because of the limited stores of ATP-CP and their rapid utilization at these high power outputs, exercise duration is very limited. Even though it has been shown that the initiation of glycolysis occurs early in the transition from rest to heavy exercise (Gollnick & Hermansen, 1973), muscle LA rises to only 3 mM after 10 sec and there is little accumulation of LA in the blood. In agreement with Bar-Or (1981), we would classify the maximal power output in 5 sec as the "anaerobic power."

Table 1

Proposed Classification of Activity

Classification	Approximate duration	General description
Anaerobic power	1-10 sec	Associated with amount of ATP & CP and their rate of degradation
Anaerobic capacity	20-45 sec	Same as above, plus rate of anaerobic glycolysis
Lactic acid tolerance	1-8 min	Tolerance to high levels of lactic acid
Aerobic	10 min +	Predominantly aerobic

Putting all these facts together, a new system is proposed for classifying activity (Table 1). This system assumes that the power output is the maximal amount that can be generated for a given duration; the durations, however, must be approximate. The proposed classification should make it easier to understand and evaluate the various anaerobic tests available and the effects of different training programs on anaerobic performance.

ANAEROBIC TESTS

Looking at the variety of anaerobic tests, several points can be made. First, tests tend to be reliable in well motivated subjects. Based on their names and descriptions, however, there is not a great deal of agreement as to what they measure. Third, all tests involve high-intensity exercise of differing duration; it is this variation in performance time that distinguishes tests from one another and allows them to be classified.

Anaerobic Power

Table 2 shows examples of the anaerobic power tests lasting approximately 1 to 10 sec. These tests involve running up stairs (Margaria, Aghemo, & Rovelli, 1966), short sprints (Fox & Mathews, 1974), jumping (Davies, 1971; Fox & Mathews, 1974), contracting large muscle groups at maximal velocities (Komi, Rusko, Vos, & Vihko, 1977; Thorstensson, Hultén, von Döbeln, & Karlsson, 1976) or pedaling (fastest 4 to 5 sec in a test lasting 30-40 sec) against a high resistance on a cycle ergometer (Bar-Or, 1983; Crielaard & Pirnay, 1981; Weltman, Moffatt, & Stamford, 1978).

Table 2

Types of Anaerobic Power Tests

Test	Approximate duration (sec)
Margaria step test	2- 4
Vertical jump	< 1
Leg extensor force	1- 2
Short sprints	3-10
Bicycle ergometer (Max RPM)	
Resistance:	
4-7 kg	2- 5
4 kg (40-sec test)	4-sec max
75 gm/kg body wt. (30-sec test)	5-sec max

Anaerobic Capacity

Examples of anaerobic capacity tests lasting 20-60 sec can be seen in Table 3. With the exception of long sprints (Fox & Mathews, 1974), which are field tests requiring little equipment, most tests use cycle ergometers or treadmills. Measurements include (a) time to exhaustion against a given resistance on the bicycle (DeBruyn-Prévost & Lefèbvre, 1980) or at a given speed and grade on the treadmill (Cunningham & Faulkner, 1969; Houston & Thomson, 1977; Roberts, Billeter, & Howald, 1982; Sjödin, Thorstensson, Frith, & Karlsson, 1976) or (b) total power output on the bicycle ergometer within a specified time period (Szögÿ & Cherebetiu, 1974).

The Wingate Test (Bar-Or, 1983) is a good example of the latter type, as it measures the total power output of the arms or legs (i.e., maximal pedal revolutions) during a 30-sec bicycle test. Campbell, Bonen, Kirby, and Belcastro (1979) determined the total pedal revolutions during two 20-sec tests at 75% and 150% $\dot{V}O_2$ max, while Katch, Weltman, Martin, and Gray (1977) and Weltman, Moffatt, and Stamford (1978) did the same during 30-40 sec against a resistance of 4 to 6 kilograms. In addition to these tests in which performance was measured by the amount of exercise accomplished, others have used the maximal oxygen debt as an index of anaerobic capacity (Volkov, Shirkovets, & Borilkevich, (1975), in that it is an estimate of the total amount of energy liberated by the anaerobic metabolism. There could be some question as to whether the maximal oxygen debt should be classified with anaerobic capacity or as an index of lactate tolerance.

Table 3

Types of Anaerobic Capacity Tests

A. Maximal oxygen debt (liters)

B. Bicycle ergometer	Resistance or power output	RPM	Duration (sec)
1. Arms	50 gm/kg body wt	Max	30
2. Legs			
a) To exhaustion	350-400 W	104-128	40-45
b) Fixed duration	1.5 × $\dot{V}O_2$max	Max	20
	0.75 × $\dot{V}O_2$max	Max	20
	75 gm/kg body wt	Max	30
	4-6 kg	Max	30-40

C. Treadmill run to exhaustion	Speed (mph)	Grade (%)	Duration (sec)
	7-8	20	30-60
	10	15	35-45
	Individually designed to elicit exhaustion in 45 sec		35-60

The Wingate Test appears to have been studied the most relative to its validity and reliability. As well, norms have been established for various ages and groups, and extensive research has been carried out on the effects of such factors as warm-up, environment, and training on the test results (Bar-Or, 1983).

Lactate Tolerance

Examples of bicycle ergometer and treadmill tests of lactate tolerance can be seen in Table 4; these tests generally run 75-120 sec. Banister & Wqo (1978) found that male subjects could pedal for approximately 125 sec breathing normal air but only 65 sec while breathing 12% oxygen. The females studied by Ready, Eynon, and Cunningham (1981), on the other hand, could pedal only 75-95 sec at the same power output. Katch, Weltman, and Traeger (1976) had subjects pedal at maximum and at 80-90% maximal speed against a high resistance to determine which cycling strategy produced more power over 2 min. Although there was no difference in power output during the second min with either pacing strategy, all-out pedaling resulted in higher values during the first 30 sec and pedaling at 80-90% of maximal speed produced higher power outputs from 30 to 60 sec.

On the treadmill, Fox, Bartels, Klinzing, and Ragg (1977) found that subjects could run for about 2 min at 10-14 km/hr, 10% grade, while Kindermann, Schnabel, Schmitt,

Table 4

Types of Lactate Tolerance Tests

A. Bicycle ergometer	Resistance or power output		RPM	Duration (sec)
Normoxia (21% O_2)	300 W		100	125
Hypoxia (12% O_2)	300 W		100	65
	300 W		55-65	75-95
	34 kg/rev		Max	120
	34 kg/rev		97	120
B. Treadmill run to exhaustion	Speed (km/hr)	Grade (%)		Duration (sec)
	10-14	10		120
	20	5		75-115
C. Running, cycling, swimming, etc.	Speed			Duration (sec)
	Several speeds designed to produce blood lactates from 4 mM to near maximum			50-480

Biro, Cassens, and Weber (1982) reported a wider performance range at a faster speed and lower incline.

Using results from sporting events lasting from about 1 to 8 min, Mader, Heck, and Hollmann (1978) had athletes run, swim, and cycle the same distance as their competitive event at several submaximal speeds. These speeds were designed to produce blood LA levels above 4 mM but below those usually attained during competition. Because of the linear relationship between LA and speed at these intensities, they could then extrapolate the LA values to the maximal level after competition and estimate the maximal speed at which the athlete should be able to perform. These results were then used to control training intensity by selecting speeds associated with a predetermined LA level. Results also were used to estimate the effects of training without requiring the athlete to perform maximally. In other words, if the athlete improved, LA at a given speed would drop and the extrapolated line would shift to the right, indicating that the athlete should be able to run, swim, or cycle faster at the same maximal LA. Conversely, if the athlete was overtrained, LA at the given speed would be higher and the training program could be adjusted.

TRAINING AND ANAEROBIC PERFORMANCE

Effects of Specific Programs

General characteristics of anaerobic training programs are listed in Table 5. Except for programs designed to increase strength, most use interval programs of running or cycling at maximal or near-maximal intensities.

Summarizing the effect of training on anaerobic performance is both complex and simple. It is complex due to the many types of programs (e.g., differences in the number of repetitions, in the duration of the work and rest periods, and in the ratio of work to rest) and many tests of anaerobic performance (e.g., differences in tests used, as well as in measuring techniques and sampling times of LA). On the other hand, using the proposed system to classify exercise of maximal or near-maximal intensity by its duration, it can be relatively simple.

Table 5

General Characteristics of Anaerobic Training Programs

Type:	Interval training
Frequency:	3-5 days per week
Intensity:	Maximal or near-maximal
Duration:	5-8 or more weeks
Mode:	Level and graded running, cycling and strength

Anaerobic Power (AnP). Looking at the first two studies in Table 6 (Thorstensson, Sjödin, & Karlsson, 1975; Thorstensson et al., 1976), in which the duration of the exercise bouts was 5 and 10 to 12 sec, respectively, both reported significant increases in leg strength, height jumped, and myokinase activity. Following sprint training, Thorstensson et al. (1975) also found increases in CPK and ATPase activities, while

Table 6

Summary of 11 Studies on Training and Anaerobic Performance*

Description of training program	Duration of training bouts	Effect on anaerobic power	Effect on anaerobic capacity	Effect on lactate tolerance
1. Run 20-40 reps, 19-24 km/hr, 9-10% grade	5 sec	+	0	
2. 3 sets of 6 maximal lifts	10-12 sec**	+	0	
3. 10-15 rides, 1.5-2 x $\dot{V}O_2$ max (60 or 120 rpm)	20 sec	+	+	
4. 2 all-out rides at 4 kg	40 sec	+	+	
5. 8 200-meter runs at 90% maximal speed	25-30 sec**		+	
6. Interval sprints, 200 m 2-mile runs, fast pace	25-30 sec** 14-20 min**		+	+
7. 10 rides at 110-150% $\dot{V}O_2$ max (50 rpm)	60 sec		+	+
8. 3 × 250 m uphill runs 3 × 300-600 m runs 3 runs at 20-24 km/hr, 3% grade	30-35 sec** 40-90 sec** 60 sec		+ /0	+
9. 6 rides at 300 watts (100 rpm) in hypoxia (12% O_2) and normoxia (21% O_2)	180 sec			+
10. Up to 19 runs at 15-17 km/hr, 5-10% grade Up to 7 runs at 10-12 km/hr, 5-12% grade	30 sec 120 sec	0		+
11. 5 sprints, 44% grade 15 maximal leg presses 3 maximal runs, 3.3% grade 2 maximal runs, 3.3% grade	6 sec 30 sec** 60 sec 90 sec	+ /0	+	+

*See text for details

**Duration estimated from program description

Blank = not measured; 0 = no change; + = improvement

Thorstensson et al. (1976) found no change in these phosphagen enzymes after strength training. Although Thorstensson et al. (1975) saw no change in ATP or CP concentrations, they did find an increase in the total amount of these phosphagens due to a larger muscle mass. Possibly due to the brief duration of the training bouts, no change in LDH or PFK (enzymes involved in anaerobic glycolysis) was reported.

AnP and Anaerobic Capacity (AnC). Following 20-sec training bouts on the bicycle ergometer, Campbell et al. (1979) reported significant increases in the Sargent jump (AnP) and in the 20-sec power output on the bicycle ergometer (AnC). Weltman et al. (1978) used training bouts of 40 sec and found improvements in both the peak 4-sec (AnP) and total 40-sec (AnC) power outputs.

AnC. After subjects ran 25-30 sec, Roberts et al. (1982) reported a rise in treadmill run time to exhaustion (47 to 58 sec), no change in post-exercise LA, and increased activity of the following glycolytic enzymes: phosphorylase, PFK, GAPDH, LDH, and MDH. The lack of change in SDH activity suggests that the mitochondrial oxidative enzymes were not affected.

AnC and Lactate Tolerance (LT). With bouts involving sprints of 25-30 sec and 2-mile runs at a fast pace (14-20 min), Cunningham & Faulkner (1969) stressed both the anaerobic and aerobic metabolism. They found significant increases in treadmill run time to exhaustion (52 to 64 sec) and associated increases in maximal oxygen debt (9%) and maximal LA (17%). Similarly, Ready et al. (1981) trained women for 60 sec at 110%-150% $\dot{V}O_2$ max and found increases in bicycle ride time to exhaustion (84 to 124 sec), maximal oxygen debt (20%), and maximal LA (62%). Sjödin et al. (1976) had subjects sprint for 30 to 90 sec and reported significant increases in treadmill run time to exhaustion (47 to 58 secs) and maximal LA (10%) after the 4- to 7-min test for $\dot{V}O_2$ max. Interestingly, they found no change in LDH activity.

LT. Banister and Woo (1978) had subjects train using 3-min intervals breathing either a 21% (air) or 12% oxygen mixture. Exercise time to exhaustion rose significantly from 2 to 5 min breathing air and from 1.1 to 2.3 min during hypoxia. Even though they did increase exercise time, no significant difference in post-exercise LA was found in either condition. Subjects in the study by Fox et al. (1977) ran 30-sec and 2-min intervals. There was a significant rise in $\dot{V}O_2$ max but no difference in either the Margaria test (AnP) or maximal LA following exhaustive exercise. On the other hand, there was a decrease in LA during and after a standard 2-min run that was exhausting before training. Although not listed in Table 6, Mader et al. (1978) also report that training causes a reduction in LA at a given power output lasting 1 to 8 min.

AnP, AnC and LT. In the only study reviewed that trained and tested subjects at durations associated with all three classifications of anaerobic performance, Houston and Thomson (1977) had endurance-adapted subjects train at intervals of 6, 30, 60, and 90 sec. In terms of AnP, significant increases were reported for leg strength (35%) and concentration of ATP in muscle (15%), but there were no differences in the concentration of CP or in the performance of the Margaria test. Treadmill run time to exhaustion increased 17% (47 to 55 sec) and there was a significant rise in the average distance covered in the 60-sec (14%) and 90-sec (13%) training runs. Although there was a 14% increase in maximal LA after training, no difference in LDH activity was recorded.

Summary. Improvements in AnP with training appear to be primarily associated with increases in the amount of ATP and its rate of degradation. Improved AnC is essentially brought about by increasing the rate of glycolysis, resulting in increases in power output, maximal LA, and maximal oxygen debt for activities lasting 20-45 sec. Similarly, LT is improved with training by increasing performance time, maximal LA, and oxygen debt for activities lasting 1 to 8 min and by decreasing LA after standard workloads of similar duration.

As has been mentioned, there are many criteria and tests of anaerobic performance. Although some results may seem ambiguous and equivocal, the type of adaptation to training does appear to be related to the duration of the training bouts, that is, the effects tend to be specific to the type(s) of anaerobic performance being trained. Unfortunately, the duration of the tests was usually similar to that of the training bouts. As a result, there may have been changes in other types of anaerobic performance but these were not generally measured.

CONCLUDING REMARKS

Better tests and criteria of anaerobic performance are obviously needed. The duration of these tests should be specific to the type of performance being studied. The type of activity should also be specific to individual; for example, runners (or subjects who are trained with running) should be tested on the treadmill. It is hoped that the classification proposed in this paper will be helpful in this regard. Whether this will be the case depends on the validity of the system, that is, its ability to differentiate the effects of specific training programs and to distinguish among athletes who specialize in various types of aerobic and anaerobic performance. Validation must await further research.

REFERENCES

ÅSTRAND, I. (1960). Aerobic work capacity in men and women with special reference to age. *Acta Physiologica Scandinavica* (Suppl. 169).

BANISTER, E., & Woo, W. (1978). Effects of simulated altitude training on aerobic and anaerobic power. *European Journal of Applied Physiology*, **38**, 55-69.

BAR-OR, O. (1981). Le test anaérobie de Wingate—Caractéristiques et applications. *Symbioses*, **13**, 157-182.

BAR-OR, O. (1983). *Pediatric sports medicine for the practitioner*. New York: Springer-Verlag.

CAMPBELL, C., Bonen, A., Kirby, R., & Belcastro, A. (1979). Muscle fiber composition and performance capacities of women. *Medicine and Science in Sports and Exercise*, **11**, 260-265.

COSTILL, D. (1970). Metabolic responses during distance running. *Journal of Applied Physiology*, **28**, 251-255.

CRIELAARD, J. & Pirnay, F. (1981). Anaerobic and aerobic power of top athletes. *European Journal of Applied Physiology*, **47**, 295-300.

CUNNINGHAM, D., & Faulkner, J. (1969). The effect of training on aerobic and anaerobic metabolism during a short exhaustive run. *Medicine and Science in Sports*, **1**, 65-69.

DAVIES, C.T.M. (1970). Human power output of short duration in relation to body size and composition. *Ergonomics*, **14**, 245-256.

DE BRUYN-PRÉVOST, P., & Lefèbvre, F. (1980). The effects of various warming up intensities and durations during a short maximal anaerobic exercise. *European Journal of Applied Physiology*, **43**, 101-107.

FOX, E., Bartels, R., Klinzing, J., & Ragg, K. (1977) Metabolic responses to interval training programs of high and low power output. *Medicine and Science in Sports*, **9**, 191-196.

FOX, E., & Mathews, D. (1974). *Interval training*. Philadelphia: Saunders.

FOX, E., Robinson, S., & Wiegman, D. (1969). Metabolic energy sources during continuous and interval running. *Journal of Applied Physiology*, **27**, 174-178.

GOLLNICK, P., & Hermansen, L. (1973). Biochemical adaptations to exercise: Anaerobic metabolism. In J. Wilmore (Ed.), *Exercise and Sport Sciences Review*, Vol. 1, New York: Academic Press.

HOUSTON, M., & Thomson, J. (1977). The response of endurance-adapted adults to intense anaerobic training. *European Journal of Applied Physiology*, **36**, 207-213.

KARLSSON, J. (1971). Lactate and phosphagen concentrations in working muscle of man. *Acta Physiologica Scandinavica* (Suppl. 358).

KATCH, V., Weltman, A., Martin, R., & Gray, L. (1977). Optimal test characteristics for maximal anaerobic work on the bicycle ergometer. *Research Quarterly*, **48**, 319-326.

KATCH, V., Weltman, A., & Traeger, L. (1976). All-out versus steady-paced cycling for maximal work output of short duration. *Research Quarterly*, **47**, 164-168.

KINDERMANN, W., & Keul, J. (1977). Lactate acidosis with different forms of sports activities. *Canadian Journal of Applied Sport Sciences*, **2**, 177-182.

KINDERMANN, W., Schnabel, A., Schmitt, W., Biro, G., Cassens, J., & Weber, F. (1982). Catecholamines, growth hormone, cortisol, insulin, and sex hormones in anaerobic and aerobic exercise. *European Journal of Applied Physiology*, **49**, 389-399.

KINDERMANN, W., Simon, G., & Keul, J. (1978). Dauertraining—Ermittlung der optimalen Trainingsherzfrequenz und Leistungsfähigkeit. *Leistungssport*, **8**, 34-39.

KOMI, P., Rusko, H., Vos, J., & Vihko, V. (1977). Anaerobic performance capacity in athletes. *Acta Physiologica Scandinavica*, **100**, 107-114.

MADER, A., Liesen, H., Heck., H., Philippi, H., Rost, R., Schürch, P., & Hollmann, W. (1976). Zur Beurteilung der sportartspezifischen Ausdauerleistungsfähigkeit im Labor. *Sportarzt und Sportmedizin*, **5**, 109-112.

MADER, A., Heck, H., & Hollmann, W. (1978). Evaluation of lactic acid anaerobic energy contribution by determination of postexercise lactic acid concentration of ear capillary blood in middle-distance runners and swimmers. In F. Landry & W. Orban (Eds.), *The International Congress of Physical Activity Sciences*, Vol. 4, Exercise Physiology. Miami: Symposium Specialists.

MARGARIA, R., Aghemo, P., & Rovelli, E. (1966). Measurement of muscular power (anaerobic) in man. *Journal of Applied Physiology*, **21**, 1662-1664.

OSNES, J., & Hermansen, L. (1972). Acid-base balance after maximal exercise of short duration. *Journal of Applied Physiology*, **32**, 59-63.

READY, A., Eynon, R., & Cunningham, D. (1981). Effect of interval training and detraining on anaerobic fitness in women. *Canadian Journal of Applied Sport Sciences*, **6**, 114-118.

ROBERTS, A., Billeter, R., & Howald, H. (1982). Anaerobic muscle enzyme changes after interval training. *International Journal of Sports Medicine*, **3**, 18-21.

SALTIN, B. (1971). Guidelines for physical training. *Scandinavian Journal of Rehabilitation Medicine*, **3**, 39-46.

SJÖDIN, B., Thorstensson, A., Frith, K., & Karlsson, J. (1976). Effect of physical training on LDH activity and LDH isozyme pattern in human skeletal muscle. *Acta Physiologica Scandinavica*, **97**, 150-157.

SKINNER, J., & McLellan, T. (1980). The transition from aerobic to anaerobic metabolism. *Research Quarterly*, **50**, 234-248.

SZÖGŸ, A., Cherebetiu, G. (1974). Minutentest auf dem Fahrradergometer zur Bestimmung der anaeroben Kapazität. *European Journal of Applied Physiology*, **33**, 171-176.

THORSTENSSON, A., Hultén, B., von Döbeln, W., & Karlsson, J. (1976). Effect of strength training on enzyme activities and fibre characteristics in human skeletal muscle. *Acta Physiologica Scandinavica*, **96**, 392-398.

THORSTENSSON, A., Sjödin, B., & Karlsson, J. (1975). Enzyme activities and muscle strength after "sprint training" in man. *Acta Physiologica Scandinavica*, **94**, 313-318.

VOLKOV, N., Shirkovets, E., & Borilkevich, V. (1975). Assessment of aerobic and anaerobic capacity of athletes in treadmill running tests. *European Journal of Applied Physiology*, **34**, 121-130.

WELTMAN, A., Moffatt, R., & Stamford, B. (1978). Supramaximal training in females: Effects on anaerobic capacity and aerobic power. *Journal of Sports Medicine and Physical Fitness*, **18**, 237-244.

Body Composition and Athletic Performance

Wayne E. Sinning
Kent State University

Considerable effort has been expended to develop methods for measuring the body composition of athletes, but very little research effort has been focused on the significance of body composition relative to athletic performance. Several questions must be answered. For example, what is the ideal combination of fat and fat free mass (FFM) for optimum performance in different sports? What is the absolute minimum weight for athletes who participate in sports in which weight cutting is practiced? What are the implications of weight control practices for immediate and long-term health? Such issues are dealt with here relative to current literature.

RECOMMENDING WEIGHTS TO ATHLETES

A primary concern in athletics is the recommendation of ideal weight for peak performance in a chosen sport. The common use of the term *ideal weight* is unfortunate in that it implies a known optimum combination of body fat (BF) and FFM. Unfortunately, the ideal relative fat content for performance or health is not known. Such recommendations are usually based on average relative fat (%BF) and FFW values derived from samples of athletes who participate in the same sport as the person being tested. Wilmore (1983) has reviewed the literature to develop extensive body composition profiles on male and female athletes in numerous sports.

Assumptions must be made when using such profiles to set target weights. It must be accepted that the average %BF reflects a desirable value relative to the physiological and biomechanical requirements of the sport. It is also accepted that averages reflect the genetic endowment for the sport and the effects of an acceptable training program. Variability of the reference sample must also be considered.

American football provides a suitable model for illustrating this concept in that the game requires a high level of specialization at different player positions. Data on professional football from Wilmore, Parr, Haskell, Costill, Milburn, and Kerlan (1976) were used in formulating Figure 1. Other investigators have presented similar data on college players (Forsyth & Sinning, 1973; Mayhew, Piper, & Holmes, 1981; Novak, Hyatt, & Alexander, 1968; White, Mayhew, & Piper, 1980; Wickkiser & Kelly, 1975;

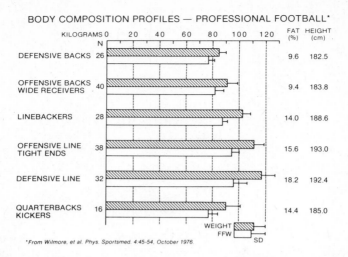

Figure 1 — **Body composition characteristics of professional football players (adapted from Wilmore et al., 1976).**

Wilmore & Haskell, 1972). However, professional athletes should reflect the highest competency level in a sport and thereby best reflect the assumptions.

Figure 1 shows that defensive and offensive backs tend to have lower relative fat content than players in other positions. These athletes must have speed and agility to execute assignments requiring quick, precise movements, as well as endurance to perform repeated sprints. The lower %BF provides a lower weight-to-strength ratio, which would be advantageous.

The positions of linebacker, offensive lineman, and tight end all involve extensive physical contact. Linebackers must react to movements of the offensive team. Their relative fat content is slightly lower than that of offensive linemen, while their weight is lower by 10.4 kg. The larger FFM and total weight of offensive linemen would be advantageous in that they are frequently involved in contests of strength with defensive linemen who tend to weigh 4.5 kg more. For the defensive linemen, the additional weight would be helpful since they must frequently react to contact by a moving offensive player. It might also be argued that the higher fat content provides some protection for the musculoskeletal system.

The relationship between body composition and the performance of runners is shown by their low %BF. Pollock, Gettman, Jackson, Ayers, Ward, and Lennerud (1977) found elite, middle-distance male runners to have an average $5.0 \pm 3.5\%$ BF, while elite marathoners were $4.3 \pm 3.0\%$ and good college runners were $6.1 \pm 4.0\%$. The fat content of 94 average young men tested by the same investigators was $13.4 \pm 6.0\%$. The elite middle-distance runners fell 1.4 *SD* below that mean while the marathoners and good runners were 1.5 and 1.2 *SD* below, respectively.

Sprinters also tend to be very lean. Barnes (1981) reported a relative fat content of $4.39 \pm 1.87\%$ for six international caliber sprinters and hurdlers. The range was from 3.79% to 8.55%. Leanness in sprinters would enhance the power output-to-body-weight ratio, an important factor when accelerating the body mass as rapidly as possible.

Female runners also present a very lean configuration. Wilmore, Brown, and Davis (1977) reported body composition data on 70 distance runners as well as 8 sprinters and middle-distance runners. Distance runners averaged 16.8 ± 5.5% BF, while sprinters and middle-distance runners averaged 10.9 ± 3.6%. In both groups there was essentially no difference between young (9 to 16 yr) and mature (17 to 51 yr) athletes. Other female athletes also tend to be very lean. Reported values for gymnasts range from 10.1 to 17% BF (Parizkova & Poupa, 1963; Sinning, 1978; Sinning & Lindberg, 1972; Sprynarova & Parizkova, 1969). Classical ballet dancers were 16.9% BF (Calabrese, Kirkendall, Floyd, Rapoport, Williams, Weiker, & Bergfeld, 1983). Snyder, Wenderoth, Baker, and Johnston (1984) found approximately 12.5% BF in elite, lightweight oarswomen. World-class female pentathletes were reported to be 11.0% BF (Krahenbuhl, Wells, Brown, & Ward, 1979).

Wilmore, Brown, and Davis (1977) noted that, in comparison to the average male distance runner, females tended to be 13 kg lighter in body weight and 16 kg lighter in FFW but 6% to 7% higher in BF content. This additional fat is an added burden that the female must carry while running. Of interest, 8 of their middle-distance runners and 7 of the 70 distance runners were comparable to their male counterparts in that they were less than 10% BF. All of these were elite athletes! Two distance runners who were only 6% BF were also the best runners in the sample.

The relationship between weight and energy expenditure has long been recognized. Margaria, Ceretelli, and Mangili (1964) found that the net energy requirement per kilogram of body weight per kilometer run was independent of speed when it was within the aerobic capacity of the athletes they tested. For level running, the cost was approximately 1 kcal/kg • min[1]1. For a marathoner, an extra kilogram would require an additional oxygen uptake of about 65 m*l* • min^{-1} while running at a world-record pace.

Studies on locomotion show that added energy expenditure for carrying additional fat is the same as for carrying an external load while walking (Goldman & Iampietro, 1962). Hanson (1973) found that changes in the energy expenditure of locomotion with experimentally induced obesity and weight loss followed normal prediction values based on total weight, including an external load.

Cureton and Sparling (1980) took advantage of such observations to develop a model to study the significance of body composition relative to the difference between males and females in running performance. They measured O_2 uptake during maximal and submaximal exercise as well as performance in the 12-min run. Males were tested under two conditions: first, without added weight and then with extra weight. The weight for a runner was equal to his body fat plus enough additional weight to give him the same proportional contribution of excess weight to total body weight as that of the proportional fat content of a paired female subject. The added weight reduced the gender difference in treadmill run time and 12-min run by about 30%, which suggests that about one-third of the gender difference in running performance could be accounted for by the relative fat content. The difference in $\dot{V}O_2$ max in milliliters per kilogram of weight was reduced by 65%. The use of added weight to study the effects of gender differences can easily be criticized. However, this is one of the few attempts to develop a model of experimentally altered body composition. More efforts are needed to develop acceptable models if we are to truly understand the role of body composition in performance.

THE PROBLEMS OF LEANNESS

The high volume training program of distance runners readily explains their leanness. However, there are other sports in which participants are typically lean, but the training routines do not require the high energy expenditure found in distance running. Barnes (1981) noted that the sprinters he studied incorporated only 2.2 miles of running per week in their training routines. He suggested that their leanness (4.39% BF) may be due to natural selection rather than training.

Sports such as gymnastics and dance, which require the controlled movement of the body through space, also typically have lean athletes. Novak, Hyatt, and Alexander (1968) reported a 4.3% BF in male college gymnasts, while we found an average of 6.5% BF (Sinning, Dolny, Little, Cunningham, Recaniello, Siconolfi, & Sholes, 1984). Reported values for female gymnasts range from 10.1% to 15.7% BF (Parizkova & Poupa, 1963; Sinning, 1978; Sprynarova & Parizkova, 1969) while classical ballet dancers averaged 16.9% (Calabrese et al., 1983). For both gymnasts and dancers, a low fat content would be beneficial from both aesthetic and performance considerations. Ballet dancers are required to have a lithe appearance (Calabrese et al., 1983).

Gymnasts and dancers follow very rigorous training routines but still need to diet to control weight. Calabrese et al. (1983) reported that ballet dancers spend over 40 hours a week in exercise. Nutritional surveys taken during the working week revealed that ballet dancers were consuming only 71.6% of the RDA in calories and were deficient in minerals and vitamins as well.

The extreme leanness of female body builders (13.2% BF, Freedson, Mihevic, Loucks, & Girandola, 1983) is of interest. Weight lifting programs do not have the high caloric expenditures associated with low body fat content. The leanness is apparently due to dietary control and aerobic exercise (Cushing, 1984), perhaps to reduce the fat covering in order to reveal the muscle definition needed in competition.

The advantage of a low fat content for successful performance in these female athletes is evident. But what about the health implications of extreme weight cutting? The frequency of secondary amenorrhea in women athletes, a condition often referred to as sports or athletic amenorrhea, is of concern. In last year's Academy meeting, Drinkwater (1984) presented an excellent review on this topic. It has been suggested that reduced body fat is a causative factor. This hypothesis, which was developed by Frisch (1976a), is very appealing. It is suggested the menstruation starts when the weight is 22% to 24% BF, and it will be maintained as long as the fat content exceeds 17% of the weight (Frisch, 1976b). Sports amenorrhea could thereby be attributed to the reduced BF.

Frisch's theory has been challenged both on the methodology of measuring body composition and on the statistical analyses used (Johnston, Malina, & Galbraith, 1971; Reeves, 1979; Trussell, 1980). Research on athletes has not consistently supported Frisch's theory (Feicht, Johnston, Martin, Sparkes, & Wagner, 1978; Wakat, Sweeney, & Rogol, 1982; Warren, 1980). Preliminary analyses of data from our laboratory on women from eight different sports showed no apparent differences between amenorrheic ($N = 10$), oligomenorrheic ($N = 14$), and normally cyclic ($N = 45$) subjects. Respective relative BF contents were $18.8 \pm 3.88\%$, $19.7 \pm 5.07\%$, and $20.0 \pm 5.82\%$. It is time to accept that low BF content may be related to sports amenorrhea, although this is almost surely not the causative factor.

Very recently, another concern about intensive training and low body weight has developed because of research suggesting significant loss of bone mineral in amenorrheic women. Cann, Martin, Genant, and Jaffe (1984) found that subjects who served as an experimental group representing hypothalamic amenorrhea were all involved in vigorous training. Spinal trabecular bone mass was decreased 20% to 30% while cortical bone was unchanged. These subjects were also very lean. Subsequently, Drinkwater, Nilson, Chestnut, Bremmer, Shainholz, and Southworth (1984) found significant decreases in trabecular bone mineral in 14 amenorrheic women who averaged 41.8 miles of running per week, compared to 14 eumenorrheic women who averaged 24.9. Respective relative BF contents were 15.8% and 16.9%.

Marcus, Madvig, Minkoff, Cann, Genant, Goddard, and Haskell (1984) also found reduced spinal bone mass in 11 amenorrheic runners when they were compared to 6 cyclic runners. However, the bone mineral content was higher in the amenorrheic runners than it was in nonexercising amenorrheic women. Respective fat content values were 10.0 ± 1.0% and 11.1 ± 2% BF. Snyder et al. (1984) found no evidence of bone loss in amenorrheic or oligomenorrheic elite lightweight oarswomen who were 11.6% BF. Loss of bone mineral content has not been shown during training in males (Aloia, Cohn, Babu, Abesamis, Kalici, & Ellis, 1978; Montoye, Smith, Fardon, & Howley, 1980; Williams, Wagner, Wasnich, & Heilbrum, 1984).

Concern about low fat content in male athletes centers around sports in which participants must "make weight." Examples are jockeys, boxers, and wrestlers. The latter group has generated the most research interest because wrestling is a popular sport in high schools and colleges. Wrestlers tend to be quite lean, but not extremely so. They tend to maintain approximately 8% to 9% BF during the season (Kelly, Gorney, & Kalm, 1978; Sinning, 1974). They then dehydrate drastically to make weight by exercising in a warm environment in an impervious garment while restricting food and fluid intake over the last 24 to 48 hours before a match, sometimes losing 10 or more pounds.

The consequences of such weight cutting may be immediate or long range. Severe, short-term starvation and dehydration has been shown to reduce isometric (Bosco, Greenleaf, Bernauer, & Card, 1974) and dynamic strength (Houston, Marrin, Green, & Thompson, 1981). Muscle glycogen stores are also reduced (Houston et al., 1981). Starvation over a 2 1/2 to 5-day period with up to 7.8% weight loss adversely affects the capacity to work at submaximal intensities (Henschel, Taylor, & Keys, 1954). However, Houston et al. (1981) did not find adverse effects on aerobic and anerobic capacity.

The effect of weight cutting on the kidney function of wrestlers was examined in a series of studies at the University of Iowa. Zambraski, Tipton, Jordon, Palmer, and Tcheng (1974) compared urine samples of high school nonwrestlers and state finalists at weigh-in. They found the wrestlers' urine to be significantly higher in specific gravity, creatinine, osmolality, and potassium but lower in pH (i.e., more acidic) and sodium. For the wrestlers, 76% demonstrated some degree of proteinuria. Later, Zambraski, Foster, Gross, and Tipton (1976) found similar results in college wrestlers. In another project, Zambraski, Tipton, Tcheng, Jordan, Vailis, and Callahan (1975) studied an NCAA championship team before a major match, collecting urine specimens over 2 days before the match and at weigh-in. Again, urine changes reflected extreme dehydration at weigh-in. Changes in the enzyme leucine amino peptidase suggested the possibility of renal ischemia. Vaccaro, Zauner, and Cade (1976) reported increases in hematocrit and serum protein showing reduced plasma volume over the 2 days before competition. Strauss, Lanese, and Malarkey (1984) found four cases of reduced serum testosterone levels in varsity wrestlers who were estimated to have an average 7.7% BF.

Smith (1980) expressed concern about anorexia nervosa and anorexic behavior in athletes. He presents a case study of a male rower who, in an attempt to weigh 155 lbs to make the lightweight rowing team, developed a food aversion and dropped from 182 lbs to 140 lbs in 6 weeks. Sinning (1978) found similar anorexic behavior in a woman gymnast. On making a college team, she weighed 56.2 kg and was 14.9% BF with a FFW of 48 kg. Two years later, after severe dieting for about 7 months, she weighed 47.7 kg with an 8.1% BF content and a FFW of 43.8 kg. Her total weight after dieting was equal to her FFW at the beginning of her career. The reduction in blood testosterone found in wrestlers by Strauss et al. (1984) was similar to reduced levels observed in male anorexics by Andersen and Mickalide (1983). The latter observed that anorexia nervosa is underdiagnosed in males.

THE CASE FOR A LITTLE FAT

Extreme leanness may be advantageous in many sports, but a higher fat content may be advantageous in swimming in that it improves buoyancy. Pendergast, diPrampero, Craig, and Rennie (1978) observed that swimming velocity is determined by two factors: the potential aerobic and anaerobic power ($\dot{E}$) and the ratio of net mechanical energy (e) per unit of drag (D). The latter is also a measure of technical skill. They also noted that the ratio of oxygen uptake ($\dot{V}O_2$) per unit of distance (d) is equivalent to D/e. By comparing $\dot{V}O_2$/d values, it is apparent that female swimmers are much more proficient than their male counterparts.

Pendergast et al. (1978) attribute this superiority to the higher buoyancy in females due to their higher fat content. With more buoyancy, females tend to swim higher in the water, which reduces D. Also, Pendergast and Craig (1974) have shown that the lower density in the lower limbs of females allows them to float more horizontally in the water. Consequently, the female swimmer can devote less energy of the leg kick to counteract the vertical component and more to a propulsive forward component.

Pendergast et al. (1978) observed that record times in pool competition shows males to be superior to females, while in marathon swimming females dominate. They attribute males' better performance at shorter distances to their capacity to develop much higher aerobic and anerobic power. In marathon swimming, technical competency is more important than power; therefore females dominate. In fact, females hold many speed records for swimming the English Channel (McWhirter & Cook, 1980).

Such observations suggest that swimmers would tend toward fatness. However, body composition studies on swimmers other than marathoners suggest that good swimmers tend to be lean. A summary of relative BF values for female swimmers is given in Table 1. For less skilled swimmers, the values fall within the range of 21.5% to 29.1% BF reported in various studies on college women as summarized by Katch and McArdle (1973). Values for more proficient swimmers range from 14.6% for the sprinters reported by Wilmore et al. (1977) to 19.7% reported by Thorland, Johnston, Housh, and Refsell (1983) for Junior Olympic swimmers. Men swimmers, for whom reported values are summarized in Table 2, tend to be quite lean. With the exception

Table 1

Body Composition Characteristics of Female Swimmers*

Source	N	Age (yrs)	Height (cm)	Weight (kg)	Fat (%)	Comment
Meleski et al. (1982)	41	17.1 ±2.4	168.2 ±6.3	56.0 ±4.7	16.2 ±3.7	Age range 11-20 yrs. Some world class.
Thorland et al. (1983)	67	15.8 ±1.4	168.2 ±6.6	58.5 ±5.9	19.7 ±12.8	Junior Olympic swimmers
Sprynarova & Parizkova (1969)	10	19.54 ±3.21	166.22 ±5.65	63.85 ±5.56	19.2 ±3.13	International caliber
Katch et al. (1969)	5			60.30 ±4.25	23.2 ±2.0	College team
Tittel & Wutscherk (1972)						
Freestyle			166.8	58.8	16.3	International caliber
Dolphin butterfly			165.6	60.7	18.2	
Breast stroke			163.5	56.2	16.7	
Back stroke			168.2	60.2	17.3	
Relay			165.5	58.7	17.2	
Wilmore et al. (1977)						
Sprinters	4		165.1 ±4.3	57.1 ±4.7	14.6 ±5.9	Level not noted
Middle distance	7		166.6 ±3.0	66.8 ±6.3	24.1 ±5.6	
Distance	4		166.3 ±5.3	50.4 ±4.4	17.1 ±2.6	

*Values are means ± SD.

of the Junior Olympic swimmers studied by Thorland et al. (1983), the means ranged from 4.95% (Novak et al., 1968) to 8.8% BF (Sinning et al., 1984), values not uncommon for distance runners.

If low density is advantageous, why are swimmers relatively lean? Their body composition is probably a trade-off between the ideal mechanics of swimming and the training routine followed to develop the aerobic and anaerobic power so necessary to compete successfully at the shorter distances. It is not unusual for swimmers to train over 10,000 meters or more per day. In addition, swimmers lift weights to develop upper body strength for the generation of power which is important in competition (Sharp, Troup, & Costill, 1983).

There is no doubt that long-distance swimmers benefit from a high fat content. In addition to the efficiency factor, fat serves as thermal insulation which is so impor-

Table 2

Body Composition Characteristics of Male Swimmers*

Source	N	Age (yrs)	Height (cm)	Weight (kg)	Fat (%)	Comment
Thorland et al. (1982)	39	17.3 ±0.9	180.7 ±7.6	72.7 ±7.4	12.1 ±1.6	Junior Olympic swimmers
Novak et al. (1968)	7	20.6 ±1.19	182.87 ±5.016	78.89 ±7.22	4.95 ±4.48	University team
Sprynarova & Parizkova (1969)	13	21.8 ±2.24	182.27 ±4.06	79.08 ±4.75	8.45 ±2.93	International caliber
Sinning et al. (1984)	27	19.80 ±1.15	178.32 ±6.41	79.9 ±6.7	8.8 ±3.2	College team

*Values are means ± SD.

tant because water stores 3700 times more heat than an equal volume of air and transfers it 25 times more rapidly. Pugh, Edholm, Fox, Wolff, Hervey, Hammond, Tanner, and Whitehouse (1955) did an extensive study of swimmers participating in the 1955 race across the English Channel. Fat content ranged from 17% to 31% on 11 male participants; the mean was 25.2 ± 4.04%. Interestingly, the competitors who finished the swim tended to have the lower fat content. It was suggested that the better swimmers could maintain a higher heat production. Consequently, they did not need as much fat to maintain core temperature.

Cold stress is accommodated by the vasoconstriction of skin blood vessels forcing the blood internally, as well as by an increase in metabolic rate. When the skin vasoconstricts, the fat acts as an insulator to preserve body heat. Pugh et al. (1955) computed that a fat thickness of 1 cm would support a difference of 1.67°C between core and water temperature in a nude person at rest. When heat production is 10 times the resting level, as it is in swimming, the same layer becomes more effective and would support a difference of 16.7°C, showing that fat is a more effective insulator at high rates of heat flow.

CONCLUSIONS

Body composition is an important concern relative to performance in athletics. However, the exact role of body composition for optimum performance has not been researched extensively. A major problem is that body composition cannot be easily manipulated, as shown in the studies on experimental obesity (Hanson, 1973). Consequently, suitable experimental models must be developed for a number of sports. Also, the immediate and long-term implications of extreme leanness and severe weight cutting to health need extensive study. We must learn more about how to measure body composition accurately and efficiently, but we also need to know more about what to do with the inrormation once we have it.

REFERENCES

ALOIA, J.F., Cohn, S.H., Babu, T., Abesamis, C., Kalici, N., & Ellis, K. (1978). Skeletal mass and body composition in marathon runners. *Metabolism, 27*, 1793-1796.

ANDERSEN, A.E., & Mickalide, A.D. (1983). Anorexia nervosa in the male: An underdiagnosed disorder. *Psychosomatics, 24*, 1066-1075.

BARNES, W.S. (1981). Selected physiological characteristics of elite male sprint athletes. *Journal of Sports Medicine and Physical Fitness, 21*, 49-54.

BOSCO, J.S., Greenleaf, J.E., Bernauer, E.M., & Card, D.H. (1974). Effects of acute dehydration and starvation on muscular strength and endurance. *Acta Physiologica Polanica, 25*, 422-421.

CALABRESE, L.H., Kirkendall, D.T., Floyd, M., Rapoport, S., Williams, G.W., Weiker, G.G., & Bergfeld, J.A. (1983). Menstrual abnormalities, nutritional patterns, and body composition in female classical ballet dancers. *The Physician and Sportsmedicine, 11*, 86-98.

CANN, C.E., Martin, M.C., Genant, H.K., & Jaffe, R.B. (1984). Decreased spinal mineral content in amenorrheic women. *JAMA, 251*, 626-629.

CURETON, K.J., & Sparling, P.B. (1980). Distance running performance and metabolic responses to running in men and women with excess weight experimentally equated. *Medicine and Science in Sports and Exercise, 12*, 288-294.

CUSHING, S.A. (1984). *Physical characteristics of female body builders.* Unpublished master's thesis, Springfield College.

DRINKWATER, B.L. (1984). Athletic amenorrhea: A review. In H.M. Eckert & H.J. Montoye (Eds.), *Exercise and Health,* American Academy of Physical Education Papers, No. 17. Champaign, IL: Human Kinetics.

DRINKWATER, B.L., Nilson, K., Chestnut, C.H. III, Bremmer, W.J., Shainholtz, S., & Southworth, M.B. (1984). Bone mineral content of amenorrheic and eumenorrheic athletes. *New England Journal of Medicine, 311*, 277-281.

FEICHT, C.B., Johnston, T.S., Martin, B.J., Sparkes, K.E., & Wagner, W.W. Jr. (1978). Secondary amenorrhea in athletes. *Lancet, 2*, 1145-1146.

FORSYTH, H.L., & Sinning, W.E. (1973). The anthropometric estimation of body density and lean body weight of male athletes. *Medicine and Science in Sports, 5*, 174-180.

FREEDSON, P.S., Mihevic, P.M., Loucks, A.B., & Girandola, R.N. (1983). Physique, body composition and psychological characteristics of competitive female body builders. *The Physician and Sportsmedicine, 11*(5), 85-93.

FRISCH, R.E. (1976a). Critical weights, a critical body composition, menarche, and the maintenance of menstrual cycles. In E. Watts, F. Johnston, & G. Lasker (Eds.), *Biosocial interrelations in population adaptation.* Paris: Mouton Press.

FRISCH, R.E. (1976b). Fatness of girls from menarche to age 18 years, with a nomogram. *Human Biology, 48*, 353-359.

GOLDMAN, R.F., & Iampietro, P.F. (1962). Energy cost of load carriage. *Journal of Applied Physiology, 17*, 675-676.

HANSON, J.S. (1973). Exercise responses following production of experimental obesity. *Journal of Applied Physiology, 35*, 587-591.

HENSCHEL, A., Taylor, H.L., & Keys, A. (1954). Performance capacity in acute starvation with hard work. *Journal of Applied Physiology, 6*, 624-633.

HOUSTON, M.E., Marrin, D.A., Green, H.J., & Thompson, J.A. (1981). The effect of rapid weight loss on physiological functions in wrestlers. *The Physician and Sportsmedicine, 9*, 73-78.

JOHNSTON, F.E., Malina, R.M., & Galbraith, M.A. (1971). Height, weight and age at menarche and the "critical weight" hypothesis. *Science, 174*, 1148-1149.

KATCH, F.I., & McArdle, W.D. (1973). Prediction of body density from simple anthropometric measurements in college-age men and women. *Human Biology, 45*, 445-454.

KELLY, J.M., Gorney, B.A., & Kalm, K.K. (1978). The effects of a collegiate wrestling season on body composition, cardiovascular fitness and muscular strength and endurance. *Medicine and Science in Sports, 10*, 119-124.

KRAHENBUHL, G.S., Wells, C.L., Brown, C.H., & Ward, P.E. (1979). Characteristics of national and world class pentathletes. *Medicine and Science in Sports, 11*, 20-23.

MARCUS, R., Madvig, P., Minkoff, J., Cann, C., Genant, H., Goddard, M., & Haskell, W., (1984, June). Bone mass in elite women runners: Endocrine and metabolic features. Paper presented at the annual meeting of the American Society for Bone and Mineral Research, Hartford, CT.

MARGARIA, R., Ceretelli, P., & Mangili, F. (1964). Balance and kinetics of anaerobic energy release during strenuous exercise in man. *Journal of Applied Physiology, 19*, 623-625.

MAYHEW, J.L., Piper, F.C., & Holmes, J.A. (1981). Prediction of body density, fat weight and lean body mass in male athletes. *Journal of Sports Medicine and Physical Fitness, 21*, 383-389.

MCWHIRTER, N., Cook, C., Matthews, P., Greenberg, S., Boehm, D.A., & Topping, S. (1980). *Guinnes book of sports records winners and champions.* New York: Sterling.

MELESKI, B.W., Shoup, B.F., & Malina, R.M. (1982). Size, physique, and body composition of competitive female swimmers 11 through 20 years of age. *Human Biology, 54*, 609-625.

MONTOYE, H.J., Smith, E.L., Fardon, D.F., & Howley, E.T., (1980). Bone mineral in senior tennis players. *Scandinavian Journal of Sports Science, 2*, 26-32.

NOVAK, L.R., Hyatt, R.E., & Alexander, J.F. (1968). Body composition and physiologic function of athletes. *JAMA, 205*, 764-770.

PARIZKOVA, J., & Poupa, O. (1963). Some metabolic consequences of adaptation to muscular work. *British Journal of Nutrition, 17*, 341-345.

PENDERGAST, D., & Craig, A.B. Jr. (1974). Biomechanics of floating in water. *Physiologist,* **17,** 305.

PENDERGAST, D.R., diPrampero, P.E., Craig, A.B. Jr., & Rennie, D.W. (1978). The influence of selected biomechanical factors on the energy cost of swimming. In B. Eriksson and B. Furberg (Eds)., *Swimming Medicine IV, International Series on Sport Sciences, Volume 6.* Baltimore: University Park Press.

POLLOCK, M.L., Gettman, L.R., Jackson, A., Ayers, J., Ward, A., & Lennerud, A.C. (1977). Body composition of elite class distance runners. *Annals of the New York Academy of Sciences,* **301,** 361-370.

PUGH, L.G.C.E., Edholm, O.G., Fox, R.H., Wolff, H.S., Hervey, G.R., Hammond, W.H., Tanner, J.M., & Whitehouse, R.H. (1955). A physiological study of channel swimming. *Clinical Science,* **19,** 257-273.

REEVES, J. (1979). Estimating fatness, *Science,* **204,** 881.

SHARP, R.L., Troup, J.R., & Costill, D.L. (1983). Relationship between power and sprint freestyle swimming. *Medicine and Science in Sports and Exercise,* **14,** 53-56.

SINNING, W.E. (1974). Body composition assessment of college wrestlers. *Medicine and Science in Sports,* **6,** 139-145.

SINNING, W.E. (1978). Anthropometric estimation of body density, fat, and lean body weight in women gymnasts. *Medicine and Science in Sports,* **10,** 243-249.

SINNING, W.E., Dolny, D.G., Little, K.D., Cunningham, L.N., Recaniello, A., Siconolfi, S.F., & Sholes, J.L. (1984). Validity of "generalized" equations for body composition analysis in male athletes. *Medicine and Science in Sports and Exercise.* Accepted for publication.

SINNING, W.E., & Lindberg, G.D. (1972). Physical characteristics of college age women gymnasts. *Research Quarterly,* **43,** 226-234.

SMITH, N.J. (1980). Excessive weight loss and dbod aversion in athletes simulating anorexia nervosa. *Pediatrics,* **66,** 139-142.

SNYDER, A.C., Wenderoth, H.P., Baker, R.S., & Johnston, C.C. (1984, June). Bone mineral content of amenorrheic/oligomenorrheic elite lightweight oarswomen. Paper presented at the annual meeting of the American Society for Bone and Mineral Research, Hartford, CT.

STRAUSS, R.H., Lanese, R.L., & Malarkey, W.B. (1984). Decreased serum testosterone with severe weight loss among wrestlers. *Medicine and Science in Sports and Exercise,* **16,** 172.

SPRYNAROVA, S., & Parizkova, J. (1969). Comparison of the circulatory and respiratory functional capacity in girl gymnasts and swimmers. *Journal of Sports Medicine and Physical Fitness,* **9,** 165-172.

THORLAND, W.G., Johnston, G.O., Housh, T.J., & Refsell, M.J. (1983). Anthropometric characteristics of elite adolescent competitive swimmers. *Human Biology,* **55,** 735-748.

TITTEL, K., & Wutscherk, H. (1972). *Sports Anthropometrie.* Leipzig: Johann Ambrosius Barth.

TRUSSELL, J. (1980). Statistical flaws in evidence for the Frisch hypothesis that fatness triggers menarche. *Human Biology*, **52**, 711-720.

VACCARO, P., Zaunder, C., & Cade, S.R. (1976). Changes in body weight, hematocrit and plasma protein concentration due to dehydration and rehydration in wrestlers. *Journal of Sports Medicine and Physical Fitness*, **16**, 45-53.

WAKAT, D.K., Sweeny, K.A., & Rogol, A.D. (1982). Reproductive system function in women cross-country runners. *Medicine and Science in Sports and Exercise*, **14**, 263-269.

WARREN, M.P. (1980). The effects of exercise on pubertal progression and reproductive function in girls. *Journal of Clinical Endocrinology and Metabolism*, **51**, 1150-1157.

WHITE, J., Mayhew, J.L., & Piper, F.C. (1980). Prediction of body composition in college football players. *Journal of Sports Medicine and Physical Fitness*, **20**, 317-324.

WICKKISER, J.D., & Kelly, J.M. (1975). The body composition of a college football team. *Medicine and Science in Sports*, **7**, 199-202.

WILLIAMS, J.A., Wagner, J., Wasnich, R., & Heilbrum, L. (1984). The effect of long-distance running upon appendicular bone mineral content. *Medicine and Science in Sports and Exercise*, **16**, 223-227.

WILMORE, J.H. (1983). Body composition in sport and exercise: Directions for future research. *Medicine and Science in Sports and Exercise*, **15**, 21-31.

WILMORE, J.H., Brown, C.H., & Davis, J.A. (1977). Body physique and composition of the female distance runner. *Annals of the New York Academy of Sciences*, **301**, 764-776.

WILMORE, J.H., & Haskell, W.L. (1972). Body composition and endurance capacity of professional football players. *Journal of Applied Physiology*, **33**, 564-567.

WILMORE, J.H., Parr, R.B., Haskell, W.L., Costill, D.L., Milburn, L.J., & Kerlan, R.K. (1976). Athletic profile of professional football players. *Physician and Sportsmedicine*, **4**, 45-54.

ZAMBRASKI, E.J., Foster, D.T., Gross, P.M., & Tipton, C.M. (1976). Iowa wrestling study: Weight loss and urinary profiles of collegiate wrestlers. *Medicine and Science in Sports*, **8**, 105-108.

ZAMBRASKI, E.J., Tipton, C.M., Jordan, N.R., Palmer, W.K., & Tcheng, T.K. (1974). Iowa wrestling study: Urinary profiles of state finalists prior to competition. *Medicine and Science in Sports*, **6**, 129-132.

ZAMBRASKI, E.J., Tipton, C.M., Tcheng, T.K., Jordan, H.R., Vailis, A.C., & Callahan, A.R. (1975). Iowa wrestling study: Changes in the urinary profiles of wrestlers prior to and after competition. *Medicine and Science in Sports*, **7**, 217-220.

Age as a Limiting Factor in Human Neuromuscular Performance

Waneen Wyrick Spirduso
The University of Texas

The inexorable march of time places limitations upon the neuromuscular performance of humans, beginning for some as early as their 20s. Fortunately, many of the physical ravages of advancing age can be postponed, through several interventions, for several years. In this paper the effects of age on physical sports performance, psychomotor skills, and limiting factors in each will be briefly reviewed. A discussion of the differential aging in motor systems and components of response speed as limiting factors in psychomotor performance will follow. Finally, two ways that can modify the aging process—practice and the maintenance of health and physical fitness—will be addressed.

AGE AS A LIMITING FACTOR IN PHYSICAL PERFORMANCE

It only take a casual observation of national or world records in any sport—running, cycling, swimming, or weight lifting, to name a few, to realize that age reduces physical capabilities. Even in the very small samples representing those uniquely talented individuals who continue to train all their lives, a systematic decrement in performance occurs across the decades (Figure 1). The rate of decline is not similar in all sports; it is steeper in those events that involve longer distances (Figure 2) or require the manipulation of heavier objects, such as the hammer throw versus the javelin throw. The American Masters Record (1982) indicates that the percent loss from age 40 of weight lifted from the fifth to sixth decade to be about 20% each decade. Stones and Kozma (1981) reviewed five hypotheses that have been used to explain differential age effects on various sporting events.

Three hypotheses are based upon well documented evidence of age-related physiological deterioration. The decrease in *energy supplies hypothesis* implies that events of short duration, such as a sprint, would decline less than events taxing the supply system for long periods of time, such as a marathon. The *energy expenditure hypothesis* suggests that performances requiring a high maximal energy expenditure, such as maximum hand grip strength, would decline at a faster rate (Moore, 1975) than those requiring low energy expenditure, such as maintaining a low percentage of maximal grip strength over a long period of time. The hypothesis that Stones and

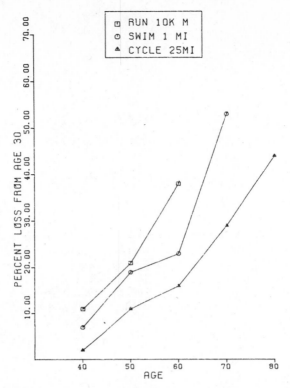

Figure 1— **Percent loss from age 30 of national record performances in running, swimming, and cycling distance races.**

Kozma (1981) found to generalize to many events and to predict more accurately was a combination of the two; performance declines more rapidly in events requiring a *higher maximal force transmission relative to the available (anaerobic or aerobic) energy* supply.

However, another physiological hypothesis that is just as plausible and is not based solely on energy supply/demand systems is the well documented change in fiber type composition of muscle with age. In a substantial number of reports of both animal and human biopsies, Type II (white, high threshold fatigable) fibers make up a smaller percent of an older muscle than of a younger muscle (for review, see Larsson, 1982). Either the threshold of large aged motor units increases to the point that they become inaccessible for recruitment in explosive types of activities, or the large motor units atrophy at an earlier age. Disuse may be a major contributing factor to the selective atrophy of large Type II fibers, as older individuals and animals tend to participate in explosive, power type movements less as they age.

Two other hypotheses not utilizing physiological deterioration constructs to predict performance decline with age incorporated sampling and motivation concepts. The *sampling hypothesis* is representative of the previously mentioned observation that selected events requiring explosive contraction and power production, for example the

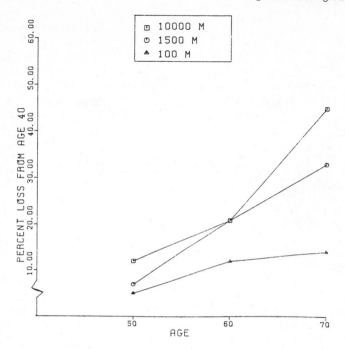

Figure 2— Percent loss from age 40 of national record performances in running events of three different distances.

pole vault, become less attractive to individuals as they age, and consequently the pool of competitors is smaller. This is documented by comparing the number of competitors in each event of Masters competition in any sport. In weight lifting, although many individuals lift weights in order to train, so few individuals in their 50s through 70s attempt the maximal lifts required in competition that it is extremely doubtful that the true capacity of older weight lifters is really known. Theoretically, smaller numbers of competitors make it less probable that truly outstanding performances will surface. The *motivation hypothesis* suggests that as individuals age, they are less prone to train hard in power events that require repetitive and strenuous explosive energy expenditure during training periods. This hypothesis is further elaborated in Riegel (1981). Neither of these two nonphysical hypotheses, however, significantly predicts performance decline.

Not only is the rate of aging effects different for different types of performances, but not all aspects of any given performance age at the same rate. Motor responses occur at different levels of complexity and depend differentially on sensory systems. It is clear that sensory and motor systems age at different rates. For example, sensory thresholds decline very little even with advancing years. Motor control systems decline at different rates that may be somewhat dependent on the complexity of the response as well as the spatial and temporal accuracy requirements for the successful completion of the response. Locomotion, which has a higher tolerance for error before deficits are seen, would appear to age less quickly than performance on a rotary pursuit task, which has high demands on the control of the motor systems involved in completing the task.

Campbell, Krauter, and Wallace (1980) have compared the differential aging effects on different types of sensory and motor efficiency in the same animals. They suggest that neuromuscular output that is the result of relatively simple integrated sensorimotor structures, such as those involved in reflex behaviors, are well developed very early in life and resist the aging process for a long time. In contrast, the relatively more complex integrations necessary to acquire and perform goal oriented coordinated behavior are not accomplished until later maturational stages and may begin declining with age in humans as early as the third decade. Campbell et al. (1980) described the relationship between level of response complexity and maturation as the "last-in-first-out" hypothesis of aging effects on motor behavior.

Psychomotor Performance Decline With Age

Neuromuscular performance that is used to communicate cognitive functioning is termed psychomotor performance. Psychomotor tests are those in which a subject signals some decision regarding a stimulus display by manually activating a reaction time key, a joy stick, or by writing a response.

In psychomotor tasks, the major effects of age are on speed of response and adaptability. In fact, the speed with which an individual can make decisions and signal them with a neuromuscular response has been termed one of the most robust and significant changes that occurs with aging (Birren, Woods, & Williams, 1979).

Long ago, Birren's group, using evidence from factor analyses of a large battery of psychomotor tasks, attributed these age differences to a large "general speed factor" that exists in older people but not in the young (Birren, Riegal, & Morrison, 1962). More recently, Salthouse and Somberg (1982b) used the analogy of fast new computers compared to an old, obsolete first-generation computer. The new computers may use "super chips" that make the same types of calculations, but at lightning speed. This new generation of computers could require the same information, use similar operations, and could conceivably use the same amount of storage, but the information processing time would be much faster because each stage is processed faster. Age differences have been reported in all stages of information processing, which include both peripheral and central processing: iconic memory, short-term memory, and perceptual processes (Birren et al., 1979), signal detection, visual discrimination, memory scanning, and temporal prediction (Salthouse & Somberg, 1982a), and choice reaction time (Rabbitt, 1980). For a review of age effects on information processing, see Birren et al. (1979) and Spirduso (1984).

COMPONENTS OF RESPONSE SPEED
AFFECTED BY AGE

An old argument that has not yet been totally resolved focuses on the extent to which age-related deterioration affects central versus peripheral mechanisms, and how these effects influence psychomotor behavior. As early as two decades ago, Weiss (1965) claimed to separate central versus peripheral components of response speed by fractionating reaction time via electromyographic (EMG) techniques into premotor latency (central; the lapsed time from stimulus onset to first EMG activation) and motor time (peripheral; the time required to activate sufficient numbers of muscle fibers to move the limb off the reaction time microswitch). Investigators have generally found greater age differences in premotor latencies than in motor times (Botwinick, 1973; Clarkson, 1978; Hart, 1981; Weiss, 1965). Depending upon the equipment used, about 75% of the difference between young and old reaction times can be accounted for by the premotor latency and about 25% by the motor times (e.g., see Hart's data, 1981).

Recently, Vrtunski and Mack (1982) reported a novel method of studying age effects on central and peripheral components of response speed by fractionating force production. Subjects maintained pressure with both index fingers on a button placed on the armrests of a chair in which they were seated. When a stimulus light was activated, the subjects pushed the buttons as quickly as possible. Activation of another light indicated if their baseline pressure fell outside the correct force bandwidth, and also when their response was completed. The response was completed when the button was activated, but the changes in force that preceded and accompanied the button activation were also recorded.

Response components were identified by determining (a) the point at which the force began to increase (premotor latency), (b) time between the change in force and the button activation (motor time), (c) coefficient p, sharpness of rise of force; (d) release time, and (e) duration of response. These measures provided not only motor time but also the amount of force that was produced and the ability to terminate force. The force parameters proved to be unrelated to the reaction time parameters. Of the several response components studied, three were independent and age sensitive: reaction time, rate of rise in force production, and the ability to terminate force. The ability to terminate force may be a capacity that is equally important in age-related decline in motor control and is a variable that has not received the attention it merits. It may be a major contributor to the problems that older individuals have in making psychomotor error corrections.

Vocal Response Speed

One type of psychomotor response that is apparently a striking exception to the universal observation of aged-related psychomotor slowing is that of vocal reaction time. When the vocal apparatus is used as the motoric expression of information processing, several investigators (Nebes, 1978; Salthouse & Somberg, 1982b; Thomas, Waugh, & Fozard, 1978) have reported finding no significant differences between the vocal simple or choice reaction times of young and old subjects. In all cases, vocal responses are considerably slower than manual responses, as can be shown in Figure 3 by data from our laboratory (Osborne & Spirduso, 1984).

Several differences exist between motor and vocal responses. Brain regional circuitry is different, both autonomic and central nervous system coordination is involved, and the fiber type composition of involved musculature is different. On the basis of apparent resistance of the vocal response to aging, proposed mechanisms to explain the effects of age on psychomotor response speed must of necessity take into account the type of motor response that is used to indicate the completion of cognitive process-

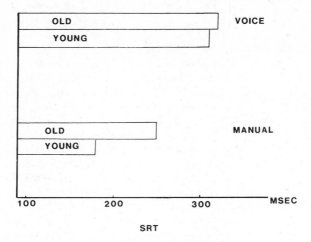

Figure 3— Comparison of voice and manual reaction times in old and young subjects.

ing. This qualification puts a strain on the notion that aging affects some general speed factor, for as Nebes (1978, p. 887) emphasizes, "Whatever the underlying cause(s) of the deleterious effect of increasing age on response speed, they do not appear to act at such a basic level that all behavioral operations are affected."

MODIFYING THE SPEED OF RESPONSE

Some effects of aging, such as arterial wall rigidity, cataract formation, graying and thinning of hair, kidney reserve, and elasticity of skin, are not modifiable. Other effects of aging, such as cardiac reserve, slowed reaction time, physical strength deterioration, osteoporosis, and skin aging, are modifiable (Fries & Crapo, 1981). The fact that many age markers can be modified through various actions reflects the extreme plasticity of our organic systems. Some aspects, such as human physical strength, can be modified seven- to tenfold by training. It is this large range of potential plasticity, in addition to huge genetic differences, that accounts for the remarkable individual differences seen in the physical capacities and psychomotor performances of older people.

Biological age markers can be modified in many ways: diet, medication, abstaining from health risks such as smoking, avoiding long exposure to sunlight, practice, and exercising daily are some examples. In this discussion, practice and exercise as modifiers will be further considered.

Practice as a Modifier of Age Markers

Practice has been reported to be more beneficial to the old than to the young in many psychomotor tasks such as digit symbol substitution (Grant, Storandt, & Botwinick, 1978), rotary pursuit (Sunburg, 1976; Welford, 1981), signal detection and memory scanning (Salthouse & Somberg, 1982a), time-on-target in two-handed coordination (Welford, 1981), and reaction time (Hoyer, Labouvie, & Baltes, 1973; Mowbray & Rhoades, 1959; Murrell, 1970; Murrell, Powesland, & Forsaith, 1962). Given enough practice, individuals over the age of 50 improve more than the young but in most tasks never completely equal the performances of the young. Practice has also been shown to benefit the reaction time of old animals more than young ones. Old animals need more practice both between and within-session test sessions to equal the performances of young animals (Gilliam, Wilcox, & Spirduso, 1984; Spirduso & Farrar, 1981).

One popular hypothesis as to why older individuals benefit more from practice in a choice reaction time paradigm utilizes the concept that the level of random background noise is higher in old than young individuals (Crossman & Szafran, 1956). Individuals have to gather data until a critical level of signal-to-noise ratio is reached at which time action is triggered, and that accumulation will rise linearly with the square root of the time taken (for review, see Salthouse & Somberg, 1982a; Welford, 1982, pp. 173-178). Differential response to practice has been responsible for contradictions in the literature regarding the effects of age on different components of reaction time.

For example, it has been widely reported that age differences in choice reaction time increase with increasing complexity of the stimulus display, yet Rabbitt (1980) maintains that when young and old are given even moderate amounts of practice, the age-by-task difficulty interaction disappears. He maintains that age differences in tasks of varying CRT complexity occur only in early practice, not in late practice. The increases in CRT with age, that appear to be a function of the complexity of stimulus display, decrease to a log constant lag when old individuals have gone through the process of neuronal statistical transactions. Statistical decision processes are the basis on which "the system" decides whether an event (Signal + noise) has occurred or whether only random background neural activity has occurred. No matter how much practice, there is always a lag constant between old and young (Rabbitt, 1980).

One of the reasons why the old may need more practice to achieve their optimum performance is that they have greater memory deficits, so the task is more novel in early stages. The obvious consequence is that single administration tests of psychomotor performance rarely provide the experimenter with a true indication of the aged individual's capabilities on such cognitive processes as visual discrimination, signal detection, reaction time, and digit symbol substitution.

In some psychomotor tasks, however, older individuals can approach the performances of the young. Given 42 to 45 sessions of practice on a small memory set, older individuals perform as well as young individuals (Salthouse & Somberg, 1982a). In a test battery of seven psychomotor tasks in which 11 components of task performance were analyzed, all subjects, both young and old, improved with practice; but only on choice reaction time and tapping between targets (Fitts paradigm) was an interaction between age and days of practice detected (Spirduso, McRae, Osborne, & Gilliam, 1984). In all other tasks—simple reaction time, digit symbol, trailmaking, and movement time—the old improved in the same ways as did the young.

Exercise as a Modifier of Psychomotor Performance

The influence of the effects of exercise on psychomotor performance has been investigated via two basic paradigms: the study of the simple and choice reaction time of individuals, primarily men, who (a) have reported that they are daily exercisers, or (b) who are tested before and after an exercise program planned and implemented by the investigators.

Almost all of the investigators taking the former approach have shown that a lifestyle of physical activity is associated with faster simple and choice reaction time (Clarkson, 1978; Hart, 1981; Sherwood & Selder, 1979; Spirduso, 1975; Spirduso & Clifford, 1978; Spirduso et al., 1984). Short-term exercise programs have not generally resulted in improved reaction times of those exercised over control subjects (Barry, Steinmetz, Page, & Rodahl, 1966; Boarman, 1977; Buccola, 1972; Tredway, 1978), but recently Dustman, Ruhling, Russell, Shearer, Bonekat, Shigeoka, Wood, and Bradford (1984) reported that a 4-month exercise program improved the performance of aerobically exercised individuals over that of flexibility and isometrically strength-trained individuals and control subjects on several tests of central nervous system function. Their experimental design was improved over previous similar studies because they included a strength exercise group as a control. They administered a battery of tests designed to differentiate the effects of exercise on central or peripheral nervous system function. As expected, they found no age or exercise effects on tests of peripheral function such as visual acuity, or visual, auditory, and somatosensory threshold. Exercise effects were seen on the tests of central neuropsychological function: recall and reproduction of verbal and auditory materials, visuomotor speed, critical flicker fusion frequency, and mental flexibility (Stroop Test).

TYPES OF RESPONSE AFFECTED BY EXERCISE

A major problem with understanding the effects that exercise might have on psychomotor performance is that the subjects are rarely well practiced; consequently the psychomotor responses recorded are from individuals who differ not only in age but in the degree to which the practice provided during the test trials has influenced their performance. In addition, the beneficial effects that exercise might have are surely different for different types of psychomotor tasks.

In response to these problems, we recently tested women of four different age groups (20s, 50s, 60s, and 70s) who were either exercisers or who were sedentary, following a similar experimental design to that used previously (Spirduso, 1975), except that 5 days of practice were provided to all groups. The tests administered were simple and choice reaction time, movement time, stationary tapping, tapping between targets (Fitts type), trailmaking, and digit symbol substitution. We calculated copy time and processing time for both the trailmaking and digit symbol substitution test.

The older women were significantly slower at all tests except movement time. As indicated earlier, practice had a dramatic effect on the performance of the subjects on all tests; except for choice reaction time and tapping between targets, all age groups improved similarly throughout the 5 days of practice. The exercise groups were superior to the sedentary groups only on simple and choice reaction time ($p = <.01$) and stationary tapping ($p = <.06$). The most dramatic difference between the simple reaction times of the exercise and nonexercise groups was in the 20-year and 50-year-old groups, in which the 20- and 50-year-old exercisers' reactions were 30 to 40 msec faster than their respective control groups. In fact, the 50-, 60-, and 70-year-old exercisers' simple reaction times did not differ significantly from those of the 20-year-old controls. The 20-year-old exercisers were also substantially faster (40-50 msec) in choice reaction time than any other groups. This was true over all 5 days.

However, by the 5th day of practice, although the 20-year-old exercisers continued to be substantially faster, all other age groups and exercise groups did not differ significantly from each other. Group comparisons of the stationary tapping results were similar to those of the choice reaction time results. The 20-year-old exercisers were able to tap almost one tap per second more than 20-year-old controls, but there were no differences between exercise groups at 50 or 60 years of age. The exercise group-by-days interaction term was significant in the digit symbol analysis, indicating that the control groups were slightly better than the exercise groups on the first day, but the exercise group means were two digits better than the control groups' on days 2 through 5. Overall, however, the exercise groups were not significantly better than the control groups on this test.

Exercise effects appeared to be significant for those psychomotor performances requiring quick perception and discrimination of environmental stimuli, as well as control of motor overflow requiring rapid initiation and termination of discrete movements. Tasks that required perceptual and/or memory scanning or short- or long-term memory seemed to be unassociated with physical fitness.

Our results extend to women the many findings of reaction time differences between exercised and nonexercised men. In addition, it appears that these reaction time differences maintain throughout 5 days of practice. We did not find differences in digit symbol substitution, as did Dustman et al. (1984), but this could be due to the different experimental design. The physical fitness level of our subjects must be inferred from their self-reported exercise patterns, while Dustman et al. (1984) directly measured some indices of fitness. In addition, our subjects had been adhering to their exercise protocol for many years, while Dustman et al. was measuring changes that occurred over a 4-month period.

Dustman et al. (1984) might have observed differences that result from a relatively acute exercise-induced adaptive overshoot in some systems that dissipates over a more extended period of time as the body chronically adapts to the increased exercise load. Since Dustman et al. also found exercise group differences in other measures of cognitive functioning such as mental flexibility and visuomotor speed, this supports their finding of differences in the digit symbol substitution test. Others have also reported effects of a short-term exercise program on another measure of cognitive function, crystallized intelligence (Elsayed, Ismail, & Young, 1980; Powell & Pohndorf, 1971).

SUMMARY

Advancing age is a limiting factor in most types of human activities that have a substantial motor component. These limitations are readily seen in sport performances such as running, cycling, swimming, and weight lifting, but are also seen in psychomotor behavior that utilizes much smaller movements. In gross body movements requiring the use of large muscle masses, the aging effect may be predicted by the ratio of energy expenditure to energy supply, or by changes in muscle composition. In smaller psychomotor behaviors the limiting factors appear to be the requirement of speed for a successful response, the complexity of information processing that has to be programmed within a specified period of time, and adaptability.

Different types of motor responses age at different rates, and both central and peripheral components of the reactive types of response age. The relative contribution of central and peripheral component aging to the decline in motor performance continues to be somewhat elusive. The fact that vocal response speed, which utilizes different muscular coordinative structures and involves somewhat different brain region control mechanisms, is not impaired in old individuals indicates that more experimentation is necessary to understand fully the role of aging in central and peripheral components of motor behavior.

Practice can modify age effects, enabling older individuals to postpone some of the age-related decline seen in performance. Practice enhances the performance of older individuals, as it does younger individuals, on most psychomotor tests. Whether practice benefits older individuals more than young individuals is dependent upon the motor behavior being tested. Exercise, which has major effects upon gross motor skills, may also be a modifier of psychomotor performance—especially performances that require quick, bi-directional reactions or simple repetitive movements with little accuracy involved.

While exercise may certainly postpone some deterioration in reaction time to the extent that older exercisers sometimes have faster reaction time than young sedentary individuals, older exercisers as a group never have reaction times that are as fast as younger exercisers as a group. Nevertheless, the degree to which age-related deterioration can be postponed in both gross motor performance and psychomotor behavior with consistent practice and the maintenance of a healthy and physically fit lifestyle is quite remarkable. The evidence strongly supports practice and exercise as ways to reduce the limitations that advancing age places upon human neuromuscular performance.

REFERENCES

BARRY, A.J., Steinmetz, J.R., Page, H.F., & Rodahl, K. (1966). The effects of physical conditioning on older individuals. II. Motor performance and cognitive function. *Journal of Gerontology, 21,* 182-191.

BECK, E.C., Swanson, C., & Dustman, R.E. (1980). Long latency components of the visually evoked potential in man: Effects of aging. *Experimental Aging Research, 6,* 523-545.

BIRREN, J.E., Woods, A.M., & Williams, M.V. (1979). Speed of behavior as an indicator of age changes and the integrity of the nervous system. In F. Hoffmeister & C. Muller (Eds.), *Brain function in old age.* Berlin: Springer-Verlag.

BIRREN, J.E., Riegal, K.F., & Morrison, D.F. (1962). Age differences in response speed as a function of controlled variations of stimulus conditions: Evidence of a general speed factor. *Gerontologia, 1962, 6,* 1-18.

BOARMAN, A.M. (1977). The effect of folk dancing upon reaction time and movement time of senior citizens. Unpublished dissertation, Oregon State University.

BOTWINICK, J. (1973). *Aging and behavior.* Springfield, IL: Thomas.

BUCCOLA, V.A. (1972). Physiological and psychological changes in the aged following a fourteen-week physical training program. Unpublished dissertation, Arizona State University.

CAMPBELL, B.A., Krauter, E.E., & Wallace, J.E. (1980). Animal models of aging: Sensory-motor and cognitive function in the aged rat. In D.G. Stein (Ed.), *The psychobiology of aging: Problems and perspectives.* New York: Elsevier/North Holland.

CLARKSON, P.M. (1970). The effect of age and activity level on simple and choice fractionated response time. *European Journal of Applied Physiology, 40*, 17-25.

CROSSMAN, E.R.F.W., & Szafran, J. (1956). Changes in the speed of information intake and discrimination. *Experientia Supplimentum, 4*, 128-135.

DORFMAN, L.J., & Bosley, T.M. (1979). Age-related changes in peripheral and central nerve conduction velocity in man. *Neurology, 29*, 38-44.

DUSTMAN, R.E., & Beck, E.C. (1969). The effects of motivation and aging on the waveform of visually evoked potentials. *Electroencepholagraphy and Clinical Neurophysiology, 26*, 2-11.

DUSTMAN, R.E., Ruhling, R.O., Russell, E.M., Shearer, D.E., Bonekat, H.W., Shigeoka, J.W., Wood, J.S., & Bradford, C. (1984). Aerobic exercise training and improved neuropsychological function of older adults. *Neurobiology of Aging, 5*, 35-42.

ELSAYED, M., Ismail, A.H., & Young, R.J. (1980). Intellectual differences of adult men related to age and physical fitness before and after an exercise program. *Journal of Gerontology, 35*, 383-387.

FRIES, J.F., & Crapo, L.M. (1981). *Vitality and aging.* San Francisco: W.H. Freeman.

GILLIAM, P.E., Wilcox, R.E., & Spirduso, W.W. (1984). Longitudinal analysis of age effects on an animal model of human reaction time. *Proceedings of the American Gerontological Society. 24*, 233.

GRANT, E.A., Storandt, M., & Botwinick, J. (1978). Incentive and practice in the psychomotor performance of the elderly. *Journal of Gerontology, 33*, 413-415.

HART, B.A. (1981). The effect of age and habitual activity on the fractionated components of resisted and unresisted response time. *Medicine and Science in Sports and Exercise, 13*, 78.

HOYER, W.J., Labouvie, G.V., & Baltes, P.B. (1973). Modifications of response speed deficits and intellectual performance in the elderly. *Human Development, 16*, 233-242.

LARSSON, L. (1982). Aging in mammalian skeletal muscle. In J.A. Mortimer, F.J. Pirozzolo, & G.J. Maletta (Eds.), *The aging motor system.* New York: Praeger Scientific.

MOWBRAY, G.H., & Rhoades, M.V. (1959). On the reduction of choice reaction time with practice. *Quarterly Journal of Experimental Psychology, 2*, 16-23.

MOORE, D.H. (1975). A study of age group track and field records to relate age and running speed. *Nature, 253*, 264-265.

MURRELL, K.F.H. (1976). The effect of extensive practice on age differences in reaction time. *Journal of Gerontology,* **25**, 268-274.

MURRELL, K.F.H., Powesland, P.R., & Forsaith, B. (1962). A study of Pillar-drilling in relation to age. *Occupational Psychology,* **36**, 45-52.

NATIONAL Masters Weight Lifting Championship. (1982). U.S. Powerlifting Federation. Charlotte, NC.

NEBES, R.D. (1978). Vocal versus manual response as a determinant of age differences in simple reaction time. *Journal of Gerontology,* **33**, 884-889.

OBRIST, W.D. (1976). Problems of aging. In G.E. Chatrian & G.C. Lairy (Eds.), *Handbook of electroencepholography and clinical neurophysiology.* Amsterdam: Elsevier, **6**(A).

OSBORNE, L., & Spirduso, W.W. (1984). Effects of age and practice on vocal and manual reaction time. (In progress).

OSTROW, A.A. *Physical activity and the older adult.* (1984). Princeton, NJ: Princeton Book Co.

POWELL, R.R., & Pohndorf, R.H. (1971). Comparison of adult exercisers and nonexercisers on fluid intelligence and selected physiological variables. *Research Quarterly,* **42**, 70-77.

RABBITT, P.M.A. (1980). A fresh look at changes in reaction times in old age. In D.G. Stein (Ed.), *The psychobiology of aging: Problems and perspectives.* New York: Elsevier/North Holland.

RIEGEL, P.S., (1981). Athletic records and human endurance. *American Scientist,* **69**, 285-290.

SALTHOUSE, T.A., & Somberg, B.L. (1982a). Time-accuracy relationships in young and old adults. *Journal of Gerontology,* **37**, 349-353.

SALTHOUSE, T.A., & Somberg, B.L. (1982b). Skilled performance: Effects of adult age and experience on elementary processes. *Journal of Experimental Psychology: General,* **11**, 176-207.

SHERWOOD, D.E., & Selder, D.J. (1979). Cardiovascular health, reaction time, and aging. *Medicine and science in exercise and sport,* **11**, 186-189.

SPIRDUSO, W.W. (1975). Reaction and movement time as a function of age and physical activity level. *Journal of Gerontology,* **30**, 435-440.

SPIRDUSO, W.W. (1984). Exercise as a factor in aging motor behavior plasticity. In H.M. Eckert & H.J. Montoye (Eds.), *Exercise and Health—The Academy Papers.* Champaign, IL: Human Kinetics.

SPIRDUSO, W.W. (1982). Physical fitness in relation to motor aging. In J.A. Mortimer, F.J. Pirozzolo, & G.J. Maletta (Eds.), *The aging motor system.* New York: Praeger Publ.

SPIRDUSO, W.W., & Clifford, P. (1978). Replication of age and physical activity effects on reaction and movement time. *Journal of Gerontology,* **33**, 26-30.

SPIRDUSO, W.W., & Farrar, R.P. (1981). Effects of aerobic training on reactive capacity: An animal model. *Journal of Gerontology, 36*, 654-662.

SPIRDUSO, W.W., Gilliam, P.E., MacRae, H., & Osborne, L. (1984). Effects of exercise and age on psychomotor performance of elderly women. (In preparation)

STONES, M.J., & Kozma, A. (1981). Adult age trends in athletic performances. *Experimental Aging Research, 7*, 269-179.

SURBERG, P.R. (1976). Aging and effect of physical-mental practice upon acquisition and retention of a motor skill. *Journal of Gerontology, 31*, 64-67.

THOMAS, J.C., Waugh, N.C., & Fozard, J.L. (1978). Age and familiarity in memory scanning. *Journal of Gerontology, 33*, 528-533.

TREDWAY, V. (1978). Mood effects of exercise programs for older adults. Unpublished dissertation, University of Southern California.

SURBURG, P.R. (1976). Aging and effect of physical mental practice upon acquisition and retention of a motor skill. *Journal of Gerontology, 31*, 64-67.

VRTUNSKI, P.B., & Mack, J.L. (1982). Microbehavioral properties of the choice reaction time response in young and old. *Behavior Analysis Letters, 2*, 161-170.

WEISS, A.D. (1965). The locus of reaction time change with set, motivation, and age. *Journal of Gerontology, 20*, 60-64.

WELFORD, A.T. (1981). Learning curves for sensory-motor performance. In R.C. Sugarman (Ed.), *Proceedings of the Human Factors Society.* Buffalo, NY: Calspan Corp.

WELFORD, A.T. (1982). Motor skills and aging. In J.A. Mortimer, F.J. Pirozzolo, & G.J. Maletta (Eds.), *The Aging Motor System.* New York: Praeger.

Selected Psychological Factors Limiting Performance: A Mental Health Model

William P. Morgan
University of Wisconsin–Madison

Exercise and sport scientists historically have attempted to describe, explain, and predict maximal physical performance in biologic terms, whereas sport psychologists have usually employed psychologic models. It is only possible, of course, to separate mind and body for purposes of discussion. The efficacy of utilizing psychobiologic approaches in attempting to understand physical performance has previously been described (Morgan, 1973, 1981), and the use of such models consistently surpasses physiologic and psychologic approaches in terms of predictive accuracy. This state of affairs is recognized from the outset since this paper is restricted to the psychologic domain. In other words, the model to be described is admittedly narrow, incomplete, and conservative. It is narrow because it is restricted to selected psychological states and traits; it is incomplete because it does not incorporate potentially relevant variables of a physiological, biomechanical, and medical nature; and it is conservative because any predictive ability generated with the model will underestimate the actual potential to predict maximal physical performance.

The primary purpose of this paper is to introduce a mental health model for use in predicting and understanding maximal physical performance in sport settings. According to Bass (1974) "Models can be simple lists of possible factors of consequence or they can be complex arrangements specifying functional relationships between variables and constants" (p. 876). Furthermore, models can be viewed as simplified representations of reality, and they are usually restricted to several specific situations. On the other hand, a theory generalizes to all cases. The research described here has relied on theoretical formulations in that the instruments employed throughout this work represent operationalizations of existing theory (e.g. Eysenckian). One objective of this work is to eventually develop a theory of sport performance, but the present work must be viewed as pretheoretical.

Starr (1971) has proposed that models can be classified into one of three categories on the basis of increasing levels of complexity, and the present model is characterized as having an intermediate level of complexity. Models of this type specify relation-

This research was supported in part by University of Wisconsin Graduate School Grant No. 131123.

ships [e.g., y = f(x)], and this type of model also predicts that specific responses will be dependent upon specific stimulus conditions. More complex models contain feedback components, but the present one does not at this point.

The mental health model of performance in sport described herein has been conceptualized in such a manner that it is readily testable. This is important since the simplest test of any model is whether or not it works. The model specifies that *success in sport is inversely correlated with psychopathology.* Another way of presenting the basic thesis underlying the model would be to state that positive mental health is directly correlated with success in sport. The model predicts that anxious, depressed, neurotic, or schizoid athletes, for example, will be less successful in sport than will individuals scoring within the normal range. The model implies but does not specify causality, it is parsimonious, and it has heuristic potential. The empirical basis for the model is described in the next section.

EMPIRICAL BASIS OF MODEL

Study 1: Elite Wrestlers—Freestyle

A series of psychological inventories was administered to 32 candidates for the 1972 U.S. Olympic Freestyle Wrestling Team on the first day of a 3-day wrestle-off, which was held to determine the 10 individuals who would represent the United States in the Olympic Games scheduled for later that year in Munich. Following the round-robin competition, these individuals were classified as first (N = 8), second (N = 9), third (N = 8) and fourth (N = 7) place finishers. The following psychological inventories administered prior to the trials were selected because of their theoretical relevance and exploratory research (Morgan, 1968, 1970, 1972).

1. State-Trait Anxiety Inventory (STAI), (Spielberger, Gorsuch, & Lushene, 1970).
2. Somatic Perception Questionnaire (SPQ), (Landy & Stern, 1971).
3. Depression Adjective Checklist (DACL), (Lubin, 1967).
4. Profile of Mood States (POMS), (McNair, Lorr, & Droppleman, 1971).
5. Eysenck Personality Inventory (EPI), (Eysenck & Eysenck, 1968).

The significance of mean differences was evaluated by means of a one-way ANOVA for each of the psychological variables, and place of finish served as the independent variable. In addition, a stepwise discriminant function analysis was performed with the 8 first-place finishers serving as the successful group, and the remaining 24 wrestlers serving as the unsuccessful group. Nine of the variables yielded by these inventories are usually viewed as negative (e.g., anxiety, depression, and neuroticism), and the successful athletes scored lower than the unsuccessful on *each* of these variables. Furthermore, the *F* ratios for state anxiety, trait anxiety, depression, tension, and conformity were all statistically significant at or beyond the .05 level. The discriminant function analysis resulted in correct classification of 77% (7 of 9) of the first-place finishers and 92% (22 of 24) of the unsuccessful candidates. If one were to predict that all of the wrestlers would be unsuccessful, he/she would be correct in 75% (24 of 32) of the cases. Since the base rate for failure was 75%, and the prediction rate was 92%, a gain of 17% was observed. In terms of success the base rate was 25% (8 of 32) and the prediction rate was 77%, which involves a gain of 52%. It is common in prediction work to merely average the absolute rates (29 of 32 = 91%), but it is probably more meaningful to express prediction accuracy in terms of the gains above base rate expectancies.

This exploratory investigation (Morgan & Johnson, 1977) was descriptive in nature, and it certainly does not permit statements of a causal nature. It is often tempting in such areas to prematurely theorize and promote interventions that may be quite inappropriate. It is not clear, for example, whether these successful athletes were successful because of their positive mental health, or whether their success led to low scores on state anxiety, trait anxiety, depression, tension, and conformity. In other words, there is no evidence in this case that lowering anxiety or depression scores would enhance performance.

Study 2: University Rowers

The Minnesota Multiphasic Personality Inventory (MMPI) was administered to 50 rowers at the outset of their athletic and academic careers at the University of Wisconsin. The investigators (Morgan & Johnson, 1978) chose to employ the MMPI in this investigation because it was administered to all incoming freshmen at the University of Wisconsin-Madison at one time, and these data have been preserved for use in research of the type to be described next. Athletic records were examined 4 years later in order to classify the rowers as successful (N = 13) and unsuccessful (N = 37). Success was operationalized on the basis of the number of varsity letters earned, and successful rowers were defined as those who earned two or three awards whereas the unsuccessful were those who earned no letters. Inspection of the mean data revealed that the successful and unsuccessful rowers differed from the outset on each of the eight clinical scales (Hs, D, Hy, Pd, Pa, Pt, Sc, Ma) used to diagnose problems involving psychological adjustment. While these differences were not large, the unsuccessful scored higher in each case. Furthermore, the unsuccessful rowers scored higher than the successful on each of the four validity scales (?, L, F, K).

The MMPI data were evaluated by means of a stepwise discriminant function analysis. The MMPI variable that provided the greatest discrimination was hypochondriasis (Hs), and the equation also included the L, Pd, F, and Si scales in that order. The resulting equation permitted correct prediction of success in 12 of 13 cases (92%) and lack of success in 28 of 37 cases (76%). The overall "hit" rate for prediction in this exploratory study was 80% (40 of 50), which can be interpreted in absolute terms or contrasted with the gain over base-rate expectancies. A comparison of these evaluative strategies has been described elsewhere (Morgan, 1979; Morgan & Johnson, 1978). The findings from these descriptive investigations (Morgan & Johnson, 1977; 1978) led to the prediction that positive mental health is an asset in sports such as rowing and wrestling, and success in these sports appears to be governed in part by the absence of psychopathology. It is imperative, of course, that hypotheses of this nature be verified empirically, and research involving replication and extension of these results will be summarized next.

Study 3: Elite Rowers—Heavyweight

The third investigation was carried out with 57 of the 60 candidates for the 1974 U.S. Heavyweight Rowing team. The 57 rowers who volunteered to take part in this investigation were evaluated with a battery of psychological inventories during the first day of the national training camp. Informed consent was obtained from each athlete, and the rowers were assured that all responses would be treated confidentially. They were also assured that these data would not be used in selecting individuals for the team scheduled to represent the United States later in world competition. The inventories employed in this investigation were the same as those employed in the first study (i.e., STAI, SPQ, DACL, POMS, EPI). These instruments were employed in place of the MMPI used in the second study for several reasons. The rationale is described in the paper by Morgan and Johnson (1978).

An effort was made to identify the successful (N = 16) and unsuccessful (N = 41) rowers from the outset. All of the psychological profiles were coded numerically, and success/failure was predicted using a psychometric worksheet described by Morgan and Johnson (1978). These predictions were carried out in a blind setting; that is, the rater was unaware of the rower's name or success/failure status at the time of the prediction. It is important to emphasize that such an approach, by definition, errs on the conservative side in a subjectively based selection process. In other words, it might be argued that the coaches' selections may not have been valid in every case. Since it is assumed that the coaching staff made the correct decision in every case, the accuracy of prediction will represent a conservative estimate. It was predicted that a rower who scored average or below average on state anxiety, trait anxiety, somatic perception, tension, depression, anger, fatigue, confusion, neuroticism, and conformity, but above average on vigor and extroversion, would be successful. It was predicted that a rower whose profile was opposite of the above would be unsuccessful.

Very few rowers actually scored in the positive or negative direction on all of the variables listed above. Rowers who generally exhibited a positive or negative profile, but who deviated on one or two variables, were classified on the basis of the overall trend. The base rate for failure was 72% since 41 of the 57 rowers were cut. In other words, if one were to predict that all rowers would be cut he/she would be correct in 72% of the cases. In this particular study the prediction accuracy for failure was 84% (31 of 37), and this exceeds the base rate by 12%. The base rate for success was 28% (16 of 57), and the prediction rate of 50% (10 of 20) represents a gain of 22%. Therefore, in both the case of predicting success and failure, this clinical method exceeded base rate expectancies by a substantial degree (12% to 22%).

The above analysis can be viewed as *a priori* since the predictions were made in advance of the actual selection process. These clinical results were compared with statistical results obtained *post hoc*. A stepwise discriminant function was performed using the psychological variables described earlier. This analysis revealed that 13 of 27 predictions of success were correct, and this hit rate of 48% exceeded the base rate by 20%. The accuracy of predicting failure with the statistical method was 90% (27 of 30), and this exceeded the base rate by 20% as well. These results are encouraging since the *a priori* clinical analysis based upon the mental health model is comparable to the *post hoc* statistical analysis. As a matter of fact, since the average gain scores for the *a priori* (18%) and *post hoc* (20%) models do not differ, this can be taken to mean that the mental health model is probably approaching its maximal potential in its present form.

Study 4: Elite Rowers—Lightweight

The 16 finalists for the 1974 U.S. Lightweight Team were evaluated 1 week prior to selection of the final 8 scheduled to compete in the world championships. The same procedures employed with prediction of success carried out with the heavyweight crew (Study 3) were used with the exception that a discriminant function analysis was not carried out because of small sample size. The predictions were carried out in a blind setting, and the accuracy of prediction was examined following the completion of the selection process. Nine of the rowers had psychological profiles that were sufficiently remarkable to permit application of the clinical prediction model described earlier. It was predicted that four of these rowers would earn a berth on the team and five would not. All nine (100%) predictions proved to be correct.

It was not possible to advance predictions for the remaining seven rowers because their profiles were not characteristic of previously successful or unsuccessful rowers. Four of these individuals became members of the national team and three did not. Inspection of the mean data revealed that the successful group scored lower on 9 of 10 variables usually judged to be negative (e.g., anxiety, depression, neuroticism), and they scored higher on the anger variable of the POMS. While anger is usually viewed as a negative construct, it might be a positive attribute in certain sport settings (Morgan, 1972). The successful rowers also scored significantly higher than the unsuccessful on vigor (POMS) and extroversion (EPI). These findings confirm the observations made in the previous three studies. Successful athletes were found to differ psychologically from unsuccessful athletes from the outset in a national camp designed to identify the best group for international competition. It is important to remember that all predictions were performed in a blind setting, and success was associated with positive mental health (Morgan & Johnson, 1978).

Study 5: Elite Wrestlers—Freestyle

Sixteen of the 20 finalists for the 1976 U.S. Olympic Freestyle Wrestling Team volunteered to participate in this investigation. The analysis was based upon a comparison of the 8 successful and the 8 unsuccessful candidates from this group of 16 finalists. Since the results of this investigation have only been summarized in graphic form previously (Morgan, 1979), the actual descriptive statistics are presented in Table 1. It will be noted that the successful wrestlers scored lower on 8 of the 9 variables usually regarded as undesirable (e.g., anxiety, depression, neuroticism), but the two groups did not differ on conformity (EPI lie scale). The successful group scored higher on vigor as the model predicts, and this group also scored higher on extroversion. While earlier literature supports high scores on extroversion as desirable, more recent research fails to support this view. It is more likely that an introverted personality is a deficit in sport. In the present case, the successful wrestlers scored near the population mean whereas the unsuccessful scored in the introverted direction. In other words, the successful were neither introverts nor extroverts; rather, they were neutroverts.

Table 1

**Means and Standard Deviations for Successful
and Unsuccessful Candidates for the 1976 U.S. Freestyle Wrestling Team
on Selected Psychological States and Traits.**

Variables**	Successful N = 8		Unsuccessful N = 8	
	M	SD	M	SD
State anxiety*	33.38	5.73	42.25	9.65
Trait anxiety	31.50	3.70	34.25	10.36
Tension*	8.38	3.66	12.88	3.31
Depression	4.38	5.07	10.13	11.12
Anger	5.00	3.42	8.13	8.22
Vigor*	22.37	2.20	17.00	6.50
Fatigue	8.22	5.39	11.63	6.30
Confusion*	4.13	2.80	7.50	4.60
Extroversion	11.25	4.23	7.63	2.62
Neuroticism	8.14	5.37	12.86	4.30
Conformity	3.00	1.41	3.00	2.58

*$P<.05$
**See footnote 1.

Prediction of success with the clinical prediction model was accurate for seven of the eight cases (88%), whereas prediction of failure was correct in six of the eight cases (75%). Since the base rate was 50% in both cases, the resulting gains were 38% for success and 25% for failure. Therefore, the results confirm the findings of the previous four studies, and this replication serves to strengthen the view that *positive mental health* enhances the likelihood of success in sport.[1]

Study 6: Distance Runners

The same battery of psychological inventories (STAI, SPQ, DACL, POMS) employed in the previous studies was administered to 27 distance runners. At the time of this testing each athlete was regarded as an outstanding college distance runner or an elite, world-class performer. The purpose of this investigation (Morgan & Pollock, 1977) was not to compare successful and unsuccessful athletes, as done in the previous studies. All of the athletes in this study could be regarded as successful in one way or another.

---

[1]We have found that computation of a global mood score based upon the POMS is quite useful. This is accomplished by summing the negative scales of the POMS (tension, depression, anger, fatigue, and confusion) and subtracting the vigor score. If the POMS data in Table 1 were collapsed in this manner, global mood scores of 10.8 and 29.2 would result for the successful and unsuccessful groups, respectively. While both values fall within normal limits, the mean score of the unsuccessful athletes is three times greater than that of the successful.

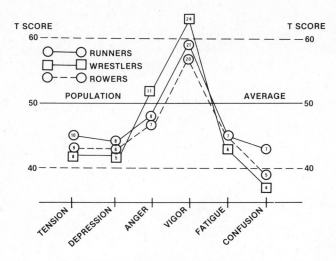

PROFILE OF MOOD STATES (POMS)

Figure 1—Psychological characteristics ("iceberg profile") of elite runners, wrestlers, and rowers as measured by the Profile of Mood States (POMS).

Furthermore, they were not competing in a specific Olympic trial or race, and their competitive distances varied from 1,500 meters to 42.2 kilometers. Hence, the present study merely permitted a descriptive analysis, and the psychologic characterization of this group is depicted in Figure 1 along with a summary of the psychologic profiles of the rowers and wrestlers described in the earlier studies.

This illustration is limited to results obtained from the Profile of Mood States (POMS), but the runners did not differ from rowers or wrestlers on any of the remaining variables. It will be noted that these runners scored below the population average on tension, depression, anger, fatigue, and confusion, and they scored above the population average on vigor. Also the runners, wrestlers, and rowers tested in these investigations possessed comparable psychologic profiles. Indeed, it is clear that these athlete groups are more alike than not, and collectively they are characterized by positive mental health.

The profile summarized in Figure 1 has been labeled the iceberg profile since its shape resembles an iceberg. That is, these successful athletes tend to score below the population average on measures of negative affect (e.g., tension, depression, fatigue, and confusion), but above average on the single positive measure (i.e., vigor). These results, while admittedly cross-sectional, offer further support for the mental health model.

Study 7: Psychopathology and Performance—College Athletes

With the exception of the second study reported in this paper, all of the investigations have focused on the study of elite performers. A more recent report by Johnson and

Morgan (1981) dealt with the personality characteristics of college athletes in different sports. The MMPI was administered to 735 male athletes from 13 intercollegiate sports during the first week of their freshman year. Successful athletes were defined as those individuals who subsequently earned two or three varsity letters (N = 197); those athletes who received one or no varsity award were classified as unsuccessful (N = 538) in this investigation. The unsuccessful athletes scored higher on 13 of the 14 MMPI scales, and four of the univariate F ratios (Hs, Hy, Pd, Sc) were statistically significant at or beyond the .05 level. However, even though statistically significant, these differences were rather small.

It is recognized in work involving prediction that use of extreme scores can sometimes be quite effective even though criterion groups (e.g., success/fail) may not differ on the dependent measures. Furthermore, there are many instances when one's concern may be restricted to the extreme case rather than the group or average case. In this study it was found that sizeable differences existed when elevated, or extreme, scores on the clinical scales were compared. Some 247 of the 538 unsuccessful athletes (46%) scored in the elevated range on one or more of the eight clinical scales, whereas 69 of the 197 successful athletes (35%) scored in the elevated range on these scales. A comparison of the two proportions indicated that the two groups differed significantly ($\chi^2 = 6.98$, p. <.01). In other words, those individuals who were classified as unsuccessful athletes showed more signs of maladjustment at the outset of their college careers than did those athletes who were later judged to be successful. Furthermore, the differences were the most pronounced on the psychopathic deviate scale, and twice as many unsuccessful (11%) as successful (5%) athletes had elevated scores on this scale (p. <.05). Elevations on the Pd scale suggest a history of conflict with others and nonconformity.

It is also possible to enhance the effectiveness of MMPI scores by notation of profile patterns. The unsuccessful athletes (6%) had elevations on both the Pd and Sc scales (48 profile code) more frequently than did the successful athletes (2%), and this threefold difference was statistically significant (p. <.05). Individuals who score high on Pd and Sc have been characterized as unpredictable, impulsive, and nonconforming. Also, their education and work histories tend to be associated with low achievement, uneven performance, and marginal adjustment (Johnson & Morgan, 1981). It is understandable why athletes with characteristics of this nature would be less successful in a given sport than would other athletes who did not have such negative qualities. These findings agree with investigations that have demonstrated a significant relationship between emotional stability and success in sport.

Study 8: College Swimmers

The studies described up to this point consistently demonstrate that a relationship exists between mental health and success in sport. This work has been largely correlational, cross-sectional, and/or retrospective in nature. Hence, it has not been possible to consider whether or not psychological functioning influences performance in sport, or whether performance (good or bad) influences personality structure and mood state. The present study represents an ongoing research program that was designed in an effort to better understand the phenomenon in sports medicine known as "staleness." Preliminary results dealing with the diagnosis, prevention, and treatment of athletic staleness have been presented, and a comprehensive discussion summarizing this project is nearing completion (Morgan & Brown, 1983). An illustration of the general findings from this investigation will be presented next.

Men and women involved in a competitive, intercollegiate swimming program served as subjects. The Profile of Mood States (POMS) was administered to these athletes at the beginning of the fall term and readministered at 1-month intervals across the season. The findings were quite consistent and have been replicated on four separate occasions. These young men and women have been characterized by the iceberg profile illustrated in Figure 1 at the beginning of each season. As the season progresses, the iceberg profile inverts for some swimmers. There is a stepwise increase in the group's mood disturbance which coincides directly with increases in the training stimulus. Decreases in the training stimulus (i.e., tapering) are associated with improvements in mood states, and the average mood state at the time of conference championships is usually identical with values observed at the beginning of the season.

Not all swimmers in these studies have responded to heavy training with an increase in mood disturbance, and those individuals who do develop disturbances in mood do not always improve with reduced training loads (i.e., tapering). Performance decrements invariably accompany mood disturbances of clinical significance, and previous levels of performance may not return until the depression lifts. This investigation not only reinforces the earlier findings supporting the view that success in sport is related to mental health, but it also demonstrates that one's mental health appears to be influenced by the training stimulus. While this investigation does not support a causal argument, it does demonstrate that performance in a specific sport fluctuates with mood shifts.

DISCUSSION

The basic thesis underlying the mental health model described here may not seem very provocative since it merely specifies that athletes characterized as anxious, depressed, hysterical, neurotic, introverted, withdrawn, confused, fatigued, and/or schizoid would be less likely to succeed in a given sport than would an athlete who had positive mental health. In other words, the model possesses a common sense or intuitive appeal. There is also evidence that information processing involving the perception of pain and perceived exertion is influenced in part by psychopathology (Morgan, 1981). This is important since the perception of pain and effort sense are known to influence the decision to persist at certain endurance tasks (Morgan, Horstman, Cymerman, & Stokes, 1983). Furthermore, there is an extensive cross-sectional literature indicating that successful athletes tend to possess more desirable mental health profiles than do unsuccessful athletes (Johnson & Morgan, 1981; Morgan, 1972, 1974, 1978, 1979, 1980; Morgan & Johnson, 1977, 1978).

While there are a number of intuitive, empirical, and theoretical reasons why one would predict that selected psychological states and traits would influence maximal physical performance, some workers in the field of sport psychology have maintained that such measures are of little or no value in predicting behavior in sport settings. The nature of this credulous-skeptical debate has been critiqued elsewhere (Morgan, 1978, 1979), and it is apparent that neither the credulous nor the skeptical positions are defensible. In other words, the use of selected psychological states and traits is clearly effective in predicting behavior in sport settings, but the accuracy of this prediction is far from perfect. The use of such data provides prediction accuracy which exceeds chance, and prediction rates have been found to consistently exceed base-rate expectancies. However, the accuracy of this prediction (e.g., 70% to 80%) is not acceptable for selection purposes.

The mental health model described here specifies that positive mental health enhances the likelihood of success in sport, whereas psychopathology is associated with a greater incidence of failure. The model is testable, and several examples of its application are presented in this paper. There is some evidence that the model, at least in its present form, has probably achieved its maximum potential. Further advances are only likely to occur if this psychologic model is expanded to include various biologic parameters. Another possibility involves the use of psychological testing in a monitoring rather than a selection or prediction context (Morgan & Brown, 1983). In other words, there is evidence that an athlete's psychologic response to training, not his or her base-line characteristics, represents the most important issue. However, the concept of monitoring represents an extension of the basic mental health model, and it too is based upon the relationship of mental health (i.e., mood states) and maximal physical performance. There is little doubt that the evolving dynamic model (i.e., monitoring component) will prove to be superior to the initial static model. The dynamic model not only incorporates a monitoring dimension, of course, but it also preserves the static features of the initial model. However, future research and application must include biologic parameters in order for the mental health model's full potential to be realized.

For their contributions to various phases of this research, thanks go to Michael S. Bahrke, Damon D. Burton, Michele Clermont, Russell O. Hellickson, John C. Hickman, Richard W. Johnson, Michael L. Pollock, William W. Richerson, and Michael L. Ross. Special thanks are extended to the hundreds of athletes who volunteered to participate in this research, and the support and cooperation of their coaches, Wayne Baughman, Bill Farrell, Jack Gardner, and Allen Rosenberg, is also acknowledged. Special gratitude is expressed to the late Dr. L.E. Drake, who was responsible for collecting and preserving the MMPI data bank employed in two of the studies described in this paper.

REFERENCES

BASS, B.M. The substance and the shadow. (1974). *American Psychologist,* **12,** 870-886.

EYSENCK, H.J., & Eysenck, S.B.G. (1968). *Manual for the Eysenck personality inventory.* San Diego, CA: Educational and Industrial Testing Service.

JOHNSON, R.W., & Morgan, W.P. (1981). Personality characteristics of college athletes in different sports. *Scandinavian Journal of Sports Science,* **3,** 41-49.

LANDY, F.J., & Stern, R.M. (1971). Factor analysis of a somatic perception questionnaire. *Journal of Psychosomatic Research,* **15,** 179-181.

LUBIN, B. (1967). *Manual for the depression adjective checklist.* San Diego, CA: Educational and Industrial Testing Service.

MCNAIR, D.M., Lorr, M., & Droppleman, L.F. (1971). *Profile of mood states manual.* San Diego, CA: Educational and Industrial Testing Service.

MORGAN, W.P. (1968). Personality characteristics of wrestlers participating in the world championships. *Journal of Sports Medicine and Physical Fitness,* **8,** 212-216.

MORGAN, W.P. (1970). Pre-match anxiety in a group of college wrestlers. *International Journal of Sport Psychology,* **1,** 7-13.

MORGAN, W.P. (1972). Sport psychology. In R.N. Singer (Ed.), *Psychomotor domain: Movement behavior.* Philadelphia: Lea & Febiger.

MORGAN, W.P. (1973). Efficacy of psychobiologic inquiry in the exercise and sport sciences. *Quest,* **20,** 39-47.

MORGAN, W.P. (1974). Selected psychological considerations in sport. *Research Quarterly,* **45,** 374-390.

MORGAN, W.P. (1978). Sport personology: The credulous-skeptical argument in perspective. In W.F. Straub (Ed.), *Sport psychology: An analysis of athlete behavior.* Ithaca, NY: Mouvement.

MORGAN, W.P. (1979). Prediction of performance in athletics. In P. Klavora & J.V. Daniel (Eds.), *Coach, athlete and the sport psychologist.* Toronto: University of Toronto.

MORGAN, W.P. (1980). The trait psychology controversy. *Research Quarterly for Exercise and Sport,* **51,** 50-76.

MORGAN, W.P. (1981). Psychophysiology of self-awareness during vigorous physical activity. *Research Quarterly for Exercise and Sport,* **52,** 385-427.

MORGAN, W.P., & Brown, D.R. (1983, September). Diagnosis, prevention, and treatment of athletic staleness. Paper presented at the USOC Sports Medicine Council's Workshop, Long Beach, CA.

MORGAN, W.P., Horstman, D.H., Cymerman, A., & Stokes, J. (1983). Facilitation of physical performance by means of a cognitive strategy. *Cognitive Therapy and Research,* **7,** 251-264.

MORGAN, W.P., & Johnson, R.W. (1977). Psychologic characterization of the elite wrestler: A mental health model. *Medicine and Science in Sports,* **9,** 55-56.

MORGAN, W.P., & Johnson, R.W. (1978). Personality characteristics of successful and unsuccessful oarsmen. *International Journal of Sport Psychology,* **9,** 119-133.

MORGAN, W.P., & Pollock, M.L. (1977). Psychologic characterization of the elite distance runner. In P. Milvy (Ed.), *Annals New York Academy of Science,* **301,** 382-403.

SPIELBERGER, C.D., Gorsuch, R.L., & Lushene, R.E. (1970). *Manual for the state-trait anxiety inventory.* Palo Alto, CA: Consulting Psychologists Press.

STARR, M.K. (1971). *Management: A modern approach.* New York: Harcourt, Brace, Jovanovich.

The Limits of Female Performance

Christine L. Wells
Arizona State University

To set the record straight, I do not believe in limits or limitations. Instead I will attempt to strike a more positive tone and discuss physiological factors that serve to define potential—in particular, the athletic potential of women.

Many physiological factors are known to influence performance (Table 1). I have chosen to focus on a few of them in terms of two broad categories of athletic performance defined relative to the primary metabolic pathway utilized. The first part of this paper will deal with the performance potential of women in activities that are predominantly anaerobic in nature. This is defined as performance that requires briefly sustained, powerful muscular contractions that utilize the so-called phosphagens (stored ATP and CP), and anaerobic glycolysis (the lactate producing pathway). For this type of performance, I will emphasize factors under the category of body composition because I believe that category to be of greatest importance for this sort of human movement. The second part of the paper will discuss the performance potential of women in activity patterns that are primarily aerobic in nature. This is performance characterized by movements that primarily utilize oxidative metabolic pathways. These movement patterns are characterized by muscular contractions that are less intense and more prolonged (or repetitive) than in the anerobic type of movement. In this case, cardiovascular factors are of the greatest importance in terms of defining athletic potential.

Although I do not wish to dwell on the differences between the two genders in the variables in this discussion, this is impossible to totally avoid. For the purposes

Table 1

Physiological Factors That Influence Performance

		Body Composition	
% Fat	LBM	Muscle mass	Muscle fiber distribution
		Skeletal Structure	
	Height	Limb length	Pelvic width
		Cardiovascular-Respiratory Systems	
[Hb]	Total BV	Heart size	Lung capacity

81

of this paper, then, male and female differences will be presented as a reference point or springboard for evaluating what we know about women's potential for sport performance.

WOMEN'S POTENTIAL FOR ANAEROBIC PERFORMANCE

The lean body mass (LBM) refers to the muscles, bones, and organs—tissues that are quite active metabolically. These are the tissues that actively and directly contribute to human movement. The remainder, the body fat compartment, is commonly divided into two parts, that which is essential for life (and for the female, essential for reproductive function), and that which is storage fat. Unfortunately, no one has really been able to decide *exactly* how much fat is essential either for man or for woman. Consequently, storage fat is a somewhat nebulous entity. Mainly we know that women, by and large, have too much of it.

It is well known that the average adult woman has more fat than the adult man. She is more endomorphic in appearance and lacks the muscular development of the man. A great deal of attention has focused on the female athlete's percentage of body fat. This has posed an interesting question because many women athletes today are extremely lean—as lean as many active men, and leaner than some have previously believed essential. It is primarily for this reason that I stated above that we really don't know the lower limit for body fat.

Table 2 presents body composition values of typical adult men and women. Specific athletic groups often differ from the values shown in this table, being more muscular

Table 2

Body Composition Values
for Typical Adult Men and Women

Characteristic	Men	Women
Height, in.	68.5	64.5
Weight, kg.	70.0	56.8
Muscle, kg.	31.4	20.5
	44.8%	36.0%
Bone, kg.	10.5	6.8
	14.9%	12.0%
Storage fat, kg.	2.1	6.9
	3.0%	12.0%
Total fat, kg.	10.5	15.4
	15.0%	27.0%
Remainder, kg.	17.7	14.2
	25.3%	25.0%

From Lamb, 1984, p. 115.

and less fat, but that is a considerable generalization because athletic groups of men and women show as much variance as nonathletic groups. Even in groups of elite male and female athletes, the relative differences remain—athletic women are about 7 to 10 percentage points higher in body fat than athletic men. The gender difference in the fat-free body weight is approximately 20 kilograms, with the man having about 40 to 50% larger fat-free mass than the woman. For equal body size, the woman has 5 to 10% less muscle mass relative to body weight than the man (Behnke & Wilmore, 1974). This means that the size of the metabolically active tissue performing any given exercise is considerably less in the women than in the man. It is this aspect of body composition that will be emphasized here.

The muscle biopsy technique has yielded considerable information about muscle metabolism and muscle fiber distribution. While men may have larger muscle fibers, a larger muscle fiber area, and possibly a larger number of muscle fibers, there does not appear to be any difference in the relative distribution of fast-twitch or slow-twitch fibers (Costill, Daniels, Evans, Fink, Krahenbuhl, & Saltin, 1976; Costill, Fink, Getchell, Ivy, & Witzmann, 1979; Edstrom & Nystrom, 1969; Prince, Hikida, & Hagerman, 1977). This means that the size of the musculature performing any given task is less in the women than in the man, regardless of difference in body size. The women has less muscle mass per unit of body weight than does the man. Table 3 presents some information gleaned from the literature relative to muscle fiber distribution and size for female athletes.

Muscle strength is related to muscle size. A smaller muscle is generally a weaker muscle. In terms of strength or power production, it is obvious that the individual with the smaller muscle mass is disadvantaged. Women are weaker than men in absolute

Table 3
Muscle Fiber Characteristics of Female Athletes

Group	Age	Ht, cm.	Wgt, kg	% ST	ST area	% area
Cyclists	20	165	55.0	55.5[a]	5487	47.6
Field hockey	23	161	57.7	48.2[a]	4305	27.5
Javelin	21	169	65.3	41.6[b]	4864	42.9
Long/high jumpers	22	177	61.1	48.7[b]	4163	44.0
Shotput discus	24	171	77.0	51.2[b]	5192	46.9
Cross-country skiers	24	163	59.1	60.0[a] 61.0[b]	—	—
Sprinters	19	168	55.6	27.4[b]	3752	26.8
Middle-distance runners	20	166	52.6	60.6[b]	6069	60.4

[a] = biopsy from vastus lateralis
[b] = biopsy from gastrocnemius
Abstracted from Wells, 1985.

strength and also when strength is expressed per unit of body weight (Fox & Mathews, 1981, p. 365). In a review of static strength differences, Laubach (1976) reported that upper body strength measurements in women averaged 56% those of men, trunk strength averaged 64% of men, and lower body strength averaged 72% of men. Dynamic strength was approximately 69% that of men. When speed of contraction is taken into consideration, men are significantly stronger (Anderson, Cote, Coyle, & Roby, 1979). My intention here is not to emphasize the difference between men and women, but simply to make the point that the larger the muscle mass, the stronger the individual.

There is really very little strength data available from women athletes, and what is available poses a number of problems as one can see from Table 4. There is a general lack of agreement about how to measure strength, what type of equipment to use, what units to use to express scores, and of course whether to compare absolute measures or relative measures. A definitive study is needed of strength in female athletes with special reference to body composition. Also, consider that women have only recently undertaken serious weight training and body building. It was previously not considered feminine to be strong or to have muscles. Looking muscular is much more socially acceptable today. Much of the older data regarding women's strength is outmoded and should be discarded as irrelevant. Recent powerlifting records attest to this. For example, at the 1984 U.S. National Championships, 24-year-old Ruthi Shafer, competing in the 148-pound weight class, set world records in the squat (230 kilos) and the dead

Table 4
Strength Measurements of Female Athletes

Group	Variable	Score
Alpine skiers	isometric kn ext	2194 N
	isokinetic kn ext 30°	189.1 Nm Torque
	at 180°	104.9 Nm Torque
Nordic skiers	isometric kn ext	1176 N
Basketball	bench press at 20°/sec	43.2 kg
	leg press at 20°/sec	177.7 kg
Throwers	bench press	115-187 lbs
	leg press	125-175 lbs
Figure skaters	grip strength	30.5 kg
	knee extension	2257.8 kg
Pentathletes	squat	87.9 kg
	power clean	59.7 kg
	horiz. bench press	61.5 kg
	pull down	60.0 kg
	inclined bench press	44.9 kg
	leg curl	36.3 kg
Volleyball	leg ext. at 90°	73.2 psi
Volleyball	bench press at 20°/sec	40.7 kg
	leg press at 20°/sec	143.8 kg

Abstracted from Wells, 1985.

lift (235 kilos). Her combined total, including a 100 kilo bench press, was 565 kilos, or approximately 1,243 pounds, the largest total ever lifted in any weight class in women's powerlifting (Witherell & Casabona, 1984).

The same problems are encountered when we consider anaerobic power: a general lack of agreement about what that really is, how to measure it, and what the best scoring method is. Even when the same test is used by different investigators, the scoring procedures often differ enough to make comparisons difficult. As seen from Table 5, tests of anaerobic power generally involve moving the body from one place to another as rapidly or explosively as possible. It is well known that women have lower scores than men on vertical jump tests, stair running tests (Margaria-Kalamen test), and dashes.

It is my contention that individuals with smaller amounts of muscle mass per unit of body weight will not be as strong or as anaerobically powerful as individuals with larger amounts of muscle mass per unit of body weight. In large measure, a woman's athletic performance potential in events that can be classified as anaerobic will be governed by her genetic endowment in regard to muscle fiber number, muscle fiber distribution (ST or FT), and muscle fiber size. The extent to which she responds to specific training techniques for strength, speed, or power will depend largely upon her ability to maximize her genetic potential, keep her body fat levels quite low, and develop appropriate motor skills.

Table 5

Anaerobic Power of Female Athletes

Group	Variable	Score
Alpine skiers	Vertical jump	273 J
	adj. for wgt	293 J
	adj. for LBW	310 J
	Margaria-Kalamen test	1131 W
	adj. for wgt	1258 W
	adj. for LBM	1357 W
Nordic skiers	Vertical jump	260 J
	adj. for wgt	288 J
	adj. for LBM	295 J
	Margaria-Kalamen test	989 W
	adj. for wgt	1162 W
	adj. for LBM	1202 W
Figure skaters	Vertical jump	35 cm
	Standing long jump	1.98 m
Pentathletes	50 yd. dash	6.31 sec
	velocity	8.35 m/sec
Volleyball (E)	Vertical jump	52.49 cm
	20 yd. dash	3.08 sec
Volleyball (N)	Vertical jump	47.27 cm
	20 yd. dash	3.14 sec

Abstracted from Wells, 1985.

WOMEN'S POTENTIAL FOR AEROBIC PERFORMANCE

Factors important for aerobic or endurance types of performance include (a) the maximal oxygen uptake ($\dot{V}O_2$ max), (b) the controversial anaerobic threshold because that signifies the onset of rapidly accumulating lactic acid, and (c) oxidative economy ($\dot{V}O_2$ at steady submaximal load) because that determines how much a particular pace costs in terms of oxygen utilization. Since some of the same physiological variables affect these three factors, they are obviously interrelated with one another.

According to the Fick principle:

$$\dot{V}O_2 = \dot{Q} \times a\text{-}\overline{V} \ O_2 \ \text{diff} \qquad (1)$$

where $\dot{Q}$ is cardiac output, and $a\text{-}\overline{V} \ O_2$ diff is arterial minus mixed venus oxygen content.

$$\text{We also know that } \dot{Q} = SV \times HR \qquad (2)$$

where SV is the stroke volume of the heart (ml/beat) and HR is heart rate (beats/min).

The two variables I will focus on here—heart size and hemoglobin concentration—have particular significance to these equations, and consequently to the three factors mentioned above. Heart size to a very significant extent affects stroke volume, and hence cardiac output—the delivery of blood from the heart-lung complex to the muscles. The total amount of hemoglobin in the body is a product of hemoglobin concentration [Hb] and blood volume. Since space limitations prevent full development of this topic, only hemoglobin concentration will be discussed here. This variable obviously affects the oxygen carrying capacity of the blood, and consequently, the $a\text{-}\overline{V} \ O_2$ difference.

Heart Size

A woman's heart size is about 85% as large as a man's, when comparisons are made in absolute volume (Table 6). This difference does *not* disappear when one corrects for body size. When heart size is expressed as ml per kg body weight or ml per M^2 surface area, the woman's heart is still only 80 to 90% as large as the man's (Åstrand, Cuddy, Saltin, & Stenberg, 1964; Grande & Taylor, 1965). Heart size is important

Table 6

Heart Volume of Athletes and Nonathletes

	Males	Females
Athletes	860	725
Nonathletes	670	580

From Falls, 1979, p. 41.

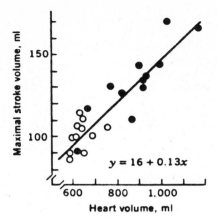

Figure 1— Relationship between heart volume and maximal stroke volume (open circles, females; closed circles, males). (From Figure 6.25, p. 172, Åstrand & Rodahl, 1970)

because maximal stroke volume is directly related to heart size (Figure 1). According to Åstrand and Rodahl (1977), stroke volume in the woman is about one-third as large as in the man.

Obviously stroke volume is an important variable in the augmentation of cardiac output occurring with exercise. In terms of maximizing myocardial efficiency, it is more advantageous to increase stroke volume than to increase heart rate (Folkow & Neil, 1971; Freedson, 1981). A slow heart rate is more efficient than a fast heart rate at any given work level. Since there is no difference between trained men and women in maximal exercise heart rate, the major difference in maximal cardiac output between the sexes is the result of differences in stroke volume. At constant load submaximal exercise, when oxygen uptake is stable and similar, it is a common finding that the woman's heart rate is higher than the man's. Much of this difference is due to the smaller heart size of the female in relation to her total body size. The individual with the smaller heart is less efficient in terms of delivering blood to the working musculature.

Endurance training has been shown to result in increased stroke volume, which is thought to be due to improved venous return of blood to the heart from the periphery. In fact, the increase in stroke volume is often one of the most significant adaptations to occur with endurance training. This response leads to an elevated cardiac output with a lessened rise in heart rate—an increase in myocardial efficiency. It is my belief that a woman's inherent heart size in relation to total body size is an important factor in her ability to elevate her cardiac output, and thus is a primary factor in her potential for endurance performance.

Hemoglobin Concentration

A second variable that seems important in a woman's capacity for endurance performance is her hemoglobin level. There is considerable variability in hemoglobin concentration within any population. In the U.S., 95% (± 2 SD) of the female population have hemoglobin values between 12 and 16 g · 100 ml^{-1} blood, while the correspon-

Table 7

Hemoglobin Status of Female Athletes

Source	Group	Hb, g%
Clement, 1977	Canadian Olympians	12.9
	Canadian nonathletes	13.6
DeWijn, 1971	Dutch Olympians	14.4
Hunding et al., 1981	runners, joggers	13.1
Pate et al., 1979	college athletes	14.6
Stewart et al., 1972	Australian Olympians	15.5
Wells, unpublished	college athletes:	
	swimmers	13.6
	gymnasts	13.3
	badminton	13.6
	track	13.0
Wells et al., 1981	marathon runners	13.7
Upton et al., 1984	middle-aged marathoners	13.7
	young marathoners	13.4
	middle-aged 10 k runners	13.6
	middle-aged sedentary	14.2

ding male values are between 14 and 18 g • 100 ml^{-1} blood. The mean values vary from source to source, but generally are about $12.5-13$ g • 100 ml^{-1} for women and about 15 g • 100 ml^{-1} blood for men (Falls, 1979; Freedson, 1981). Table 7 gives some hemoglobin values in women athletes. Since each gram of hemoglobin can carry 1.34 ml of oxygen, a lower hemoglobin concentration means that less oxygen can be carried in the blood. Figure 2 illustrates this point quite well. At a [Hb] of 15 g • 100 ml^{-1}, the arterial blood contains 19 to 20 volumes percent oxygen. At lesser hemoglobin concentrations, the oxygen-carrying capacity of the blood declines.

Since the venous blood oxygen content during exercise is approximately the same for both men and women despite differences in [Hb] (Åstrand & Rodahl, 1970, p. 161), the a-$\bar{V}$ O_2 difference is lower in the individual with the lower oxygen-carrying capacity. According to the first equation above (1), a lower a-$\bar{V}$ O_2 difference would result in a lower $\dot{V}O_2$ max. If a-$\bar{V}$ O_2 difference is reduced for any given submaximal $\dot{V}O_2$ level, then cardiac output must be increased. Both of these responses are well known. Women have lower $\dot{V}O_2$ max values than men (Sparling, 1980), and at given submaximal oxygen uptake levels women have higher cardiac output, lower a-$\bar{V}$ O_2 difference, higher heart rate, and lower stroke volume than men (Åstrand et al., 1964). These disparities remain even when comparisons are made at given percentages of $\dot{V}O_2$ max.

A more recent study (Zwiren, Cureton, & Hutchinson, 1983) comparing equally trained men and women showed both similar and discrepant results from those just cited. Men and women were selected who had been involved in a similar amount of endurance training for a number of years. $\dot{V}O_2$ max values did not differ when expressed in ml of O_2 per kilogram of fat-free weight. Figure 3a shows circulatory responses in relation to various oxygen uptake levels. At a $\dot{V}O_2$ of 1.5 1 • min^{-1}, for

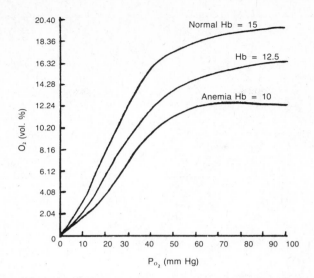

Figure 2— Oxyhemoglobin dissociation curves for various Hb concentration levels. (Adapted from Falls, 1979, p. 43)

example, there were no gender differences in $\dot{Q}$, or a-$\bar{V}$ O_2 difference, but there were differences in stroke volume (female lower) and heart rate (female higher). Figure 3b shows these same variables in relation to percent of $\dot{V}O_2$ max. At 50% $\dot{V}O_2$ max, there were considerable differences between the genders in $\dot{Q}$, a-$\bar{V}$ O_2 difference, and stroke volume with the female values lower than the male's. Only heart rates at 50% $\dot{V}O_2$ max were similar.

Freedson (1981) reported a correlation of $-.83$ between cardiac output and hemoglobin concentration in relatively active college age women at two submaximal exercise loads (54 and 69% $\dot{V}O_2$ max). This indicated that 69% of the variance in submaximal exercise cardiac output could be explained by individual differences in hemoglobin concentration. At the higher workload, the association between these two variables was more pronounced at the lower range of hemoglobin concentration. Partial correlation analysis revealed that stroke volume rather than heart rate was primarily responsible for the difference in cardiac output.

The relative importance of hemoglobin concentration, oxygen-carrying capacity, and stroke volume for endurance performance are not entirely understood. Nevertheless, it seems reasonable to hypothesize that hemoglobin concentration accounts for a portion of the unexplained variance between $\dot{V}O_2$ max and endurance performance (Freedson, 1981). The low hemoglobin values so often seen in female athletes appear to be a serious limitation to endurance performance.

In conclusion, for activities that require strength, speed, or power, the woman's small muscle mass in relation to her total body weight may be a major factor defining her performance potential. For activities that require oxidative capacity and cardiorespiratory endurance, a woman's heart size in relation to her body size, and total hemoglobin (hemoglobin concentration × blood volume) may be major factors defining her performance.

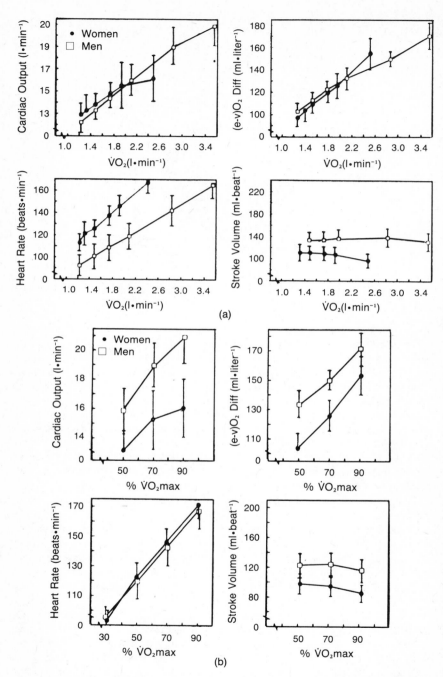

Figure 3— Mean circulatory responses to (a) oxygen uptake, and (b) % $\dot{V}O_2$ max in men and women. (Figures 1 and 2, Zwiren et al., 1983, pp. 256-257)

REFERENCES

ANDERSON, M., Cote, R., Coyle, E., & Roby, F. (1979). Leg power, muscle strength, and peak EMG activity in physically active college men and women. *Medicine and Science in Sports,* **11**, 81-82.

ÅSTRAND, P.-O., Cuddy, T., Saltin, B., & Stenberg, J. (1964). Cardiac output during submaximal and maximal work. *Journal of Applied Physiology,* **19**, 268-274.

ÅSTRAND, P.-O., & Rodahl, K. (1970). *Textbook of work physiology.* New York: McGraw-Hill.

ÅSTRAND, P.-O., & Rodahl, K. (1977). *Textbook of work physiology* (2nd ed.). New York: McGraw-Hill.

BEHNKE, A., & Wilmore, J. (1974). *Evaluation and regulation of body build and composition.* Englewood Cliffs, NJ: Prentice-Hall.

CLEMENT, D., Asmundson, R., & Medhurst, C. (1977). Hemoglobin values: Comparative survey of the 1976 Canadian Olympic team. *Canadian Medical Association Journal,* **117**, 614-616.

COSTILL, D., Daniels, J., Evans, W., Fink, W., Krahenbuhl, G., & Saltin, B. (1976). Skeletal muscle enzymes and fiber composition in male and female track athletes. *Journal of Applied Physiology,* **40**, 149-154.

COSTILL, D., Fink, W., Getchell, L., Ivy, J., & Witzmann, F. (1979). Lipid metabolism in skeletal muscle of endurance-trained males and females. *Journal of Applied Physiology,* **47**, 787-791.

DEWIJN, J., deJongste, J., Mosterd, W., & Willebrand, D. (1971). Haemoglobin, packed cell volume, serum iron and iron binding capacity of selected athletes during training. *Journal of Sports Medicine and Physical Fitness,* **11**, 42-51.

EDSTROM, L., & Nystrom, B. (1969). Histochemical types and sizes of fibers in normal human muscles. *Acta Neurologica Scandinavica,* **45**, 257-269.

FALLS, H. (1979). The physiological responses of females to endurance exercise. In D. Cundiff (Ed.), *Implementation of aerobic programs.* Washington, DC: AAHPER.

FOLKOW, B., & Neil, E. (1971). *Circulation.* Toronto: Oxford University Press.

FOX, E., & Mathews, D. (1981). *The physiological basis of physical education and athletics* (3rd ed.). Philadelphia: Saunders College Publ.

FREEDSON, P. (1981). The influence of hemoglobin concentration on exercise cardiac output. *International Journal of Sports Medicine,* **2**, 81-86.

GRANDE, F., & Taylor, H. (1965). Adaptive changes in the heart, vessels, and patterns of control under chronically high loads. In W. Hamilton (Ed.), *Circulation Vol. III, Handbook of Physiology.* Washington, DC: American Physiological Society.

HUNDING, A., Jordal, R., & Paulev, P.-E. (1981). Runner's anemia and iron deficiency. *Acta Medica Scandinavica,* **209**, 315-318.

LAMB, D. (1984). *Physiology of exercise: Responses and adaptations* (2nd ed.). New York: Macmillan.

LAUBACH, L. (1976). Comparative muscular strength of men and women: A review of the literature. *Aviation, Space, and Environmental Medicine,* **47**, 534-542.

PATE, R., Maguire, M., & VanWuk, J. (1979). Dietary iron supplementation in women athletes. *The Physician and Sportsmedicine,* **7**(9), 81-88.

PRINCE, F., Hikida, R., & Hagerman, F. (1977). Muscle fiber type in women athletes and non-athletes. *Pflugers Archiv,* **371**, 161-165.

SPARLING, P. (1980). A meta-analysis of studies comparing maximal oxygen uptake in men and women. *Research Quarterly for Exercise and Sports,* **51**, 542-552.

STEWART, G., Steel, J., Toyne, A., Stewart, M. (1972). Observations on the haematology and the iron and protein intake of Australian Olympic athletes. *Medical Journal of Australia,* **2**, 1339-1342.

UPTON, S.J., Hagan, R.D., Lease, B., Rosentswieg, J., Gettman, L., & Duncan, J. (1984). Comparative physiological profiles among young and middle-aged female distance runners. *Medicine and Science in Sports and Exercise,* **16**, 67-71,

WELLS, C.L. (1985). *Women, Sport, and Performance: A Physiological Perspective.* Champaign, IL: Human Kinetics.

WELLS, C.L., Stern, J., & Hecht, L. (1981). Hematologocial changes following a marathon race in male and female runners. *European Journal of Applied Physiology,* **48**, 41-49.

WITHERELL, M., & Casabona, H. (1984). Winners Circle. *Women's Sports,* **6**(4), 17.

ZWIREN, L., Cureton, K., & Hutchinson, P. (1983). Comparison of circulatory responses to submaximal exercise in equally trained men and women. *International Journal of Sports Medicine,* **4**, 255-259.

Heat as a Limiting Factor in Endurance Sports

Barbara L. Drinkwater
Pacific Medical Center, Seattle

Heat is a by-product of the metabolic processes that support life. At rest or during mild exercise in a cool environment, one seldom notices either the heat generated by energy transfer within the body or the interplay of the themoregulatory mechanisms called upon to dissipate that heat. During everyday activities, internal body temperature seldom varies by more than $\pm 1°$ C. However, when exercise increases in intensity and/or heat transfer to the environment is restricted, the challenge to the thermoregulatory system may exceed its capabilities, and core temperature (Tc) can reach dangerous levels.

The endurance athlete is particularly susceptible to heat injury. Within seconds a 65-kg runner can increase metabolic heat production from a resting level of ~ 85 Kcal $\cdot$ hr^{-1} to 1200 Kcal $\cdot$ hr^{-1}. If there were no means of transferring heat from the body to the environment, the limits of performance would be reached very quickly. If one assumes a resting Tc of $37°$ C and $41°$ C as the maximum tolerable level for the runner, the time required to reach that level can be calculated for any given running pace. When the specific heat of the body (0.83 Kcal $\cdot$ kg^{-1} $\cdot$ °C) is multiplied by body weight (65 kg), the result (54 Kcal) is the amount of stored heat (S) required to raise Tc by $1°$ C. Assuming a 7-minutes-per-mile pace, the athlete is producing 15 Kcal each minute of the run. Since 216 Kcal ($4°$ C $\times$ 54 Kcal) are required to reach a Tc of $41°$ C, the athlete will reach that level in 14 minutes and 24 seconds ($216 \div 15$) if no heat is dissipated.

THERMAL BALANCE

Fortunately there are avenues for heat dissipation and thermoregulatory mechanisms that serve to maintain internal temperature within a narrow range by balancing heat gain and heat loss. The classic study of Nielsen in 1938 demonstrated the remarkable sensitivity and efficiency of these physiological mechanisms. Within a wide range of ambient temperatures, Tc reaches equilibrium during light or moderate exercise as heat gain is offset by heat loss via radiation and convection (R + C) and/or evaporation (E). When ambient temperature is low, (R + C) is the primary avenue of heat loss. As Ta increases, heat transfer via evaporation of sweat becomes more important. Finally, when Ta exceeds skin temperature, heat loss by evaporation must balance heat gain from the environment as well as that produced internally (Nielsen, 1970).

The thermal balance equation describes the relationship between metabolic heat production and heat exchange with the environment:

$$S = M \pm (R + C) - E \pm W$$

where S is storage of body heat, M is the metabolic free energy production, R + C is the radiant and convective heat exchange, E is the evaporative heat transfer, and W is the work performed (Bligh & Johnson, 1973). As long as thermal balance is maintained, S equals zero, the athlete will not store heat, and performance will not be affected.

Heat exchange with the environment follows basic physical laws and varies with the temperature and vapor pressure gradients between the surface of the body and the surrounding environment (Kerslake, 1972). Behind the mathematical simplicity of the thermal balance equation is a complex interaction of physiological adjustments that involve many of the body's regulatory systems. The control of these adjustments is beyond the scope of this paper but is thoroughly discussed in several recent reviews (Buskirk, 1977; Gisolfi & Wenger, 1984; Greenleaf, 1979; Rowell, 1983). To protect the athlete against hyperthermia or circulatory collapse, these systems must function effectively over extended periods of time to transfer metabolic heat from the body core to peripheral tissues where it can be dissipated to the environment.

Immediately following the onset of exercise, heat gain exceeds heat loss and Tc rises. At one time this increase in internal temperature was considered a "failure" of the thermoregulatory process. Now it is recognized as a regulated event, necessary to fully activate the mechanisms of heat dissipation. If environmental conditions are not too severe and exercise is not too intense, the rate of heat loss will rise to equal that of heat gain and a new thermal steady state is achieved at an elevated Tc. Under some conditions of exercise intensity and environmental conditions, heat loss fails to equal heat gain and internal body temperature continues to increase. Eventually the athlete must cease activity or risk serious heat injury.

THE PRESCRIPTIVE ZONE

There have been many attempts to identify the specific combinations of ambient conditions and exercise intensities which place an individual at risk during exercise in the heat. Many of these investigations were stimulated by the need to protect workers in "hot" industries. While much of the information gained can be applied to the athlete, the work intensities in these studies reflects the average daily energy expenditure of the worker ($<50\%$ $\dot{V}O_2$ max). Nevertheless, knowledge gained from these studies has proved useful in estimating thermal limits for athletes and in identifying the individual and environmental factors which modify those limits.

The "prescriptive zone" described by Lind (1963) is based on Nielsen's original work of 1938 and was an attempt to quantify the ambient conditions in which thermal equilibrium is a function of the metabolic rate and independent of the environment (Figure 1). Rather than using ambient temperature as a measure of environmental heat load, Lind selected the corrected effective temperature (CET) as an index of external heat stress. The CET is only one of many attempts to consolidate the various environmental factors governing heat exchange into a single figure. CET values reflect air temperature, radiant heat load, water vapor pressure, and air movement (Kerslake, 1972). When air movement is minimal (<0.5 m/s), the CET is roughly equivalent to

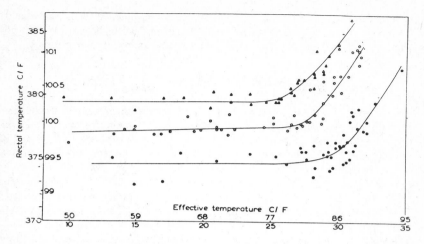

Figure 1— Thermal equilibrium demonstrated in a subject exercising at 180 (●), 300 (o), and 420 (▲) kcal in a wide range of environmental conditions. Note that the upper limit of the prescriptive zone (ULPZ) shifts to the left as exercise intensity increases. Reprinted by permission of the Journal of Applied Physiology, 18, 51-56, 1963.

the wet bulb globe temperature index (WBGT) which forms the basis for the revised American College of Sports Medicine guidelines for preventing thermal injuries during distance running.

Lind's (1963) unique contribution toward identifying the circumstances in which thermal equilibrium cannot be achieved was to extend the range of temperatures reported by Nielsen in 1938 and determine the upper limit of the prescriptive zone (ULPZ) at various metabolic rates. The ULPZ marked that point on the CET scale above which there was an abrupt rise in the core temperature at a given metabolic rate. The higher the metabolic heat production, the lower the ULPZ. For example, the ULPZ for 180 Kcal • hr^{-1} (210W) was 30.2° CET; at 420 Kcal • hr^{-1} (488W), 26.9° CET.

The prescriptive zone is useful primarily as a concept, illustrating the point that at any exercise intensity—be it light, moderate, or heavy—there is range of ambient conditions within which Tc is constant, that this range decreases as exercise intensity increases, and that for all metabolic rates Tc will rise to seek a new equilibrium level when CET exceeds the ULPZ. Under the most extreme environmental conditions, Tc will continue to rise until the athlete is forced to cease activity. Although Lind (1970) does not believe individual variability in thermoregulation precludes the use of the prescriptive zone in establishing thermal limits in the workplace, one should be cautious in using it to predict the thermal limits of an individual athlete. The concept, however, can be used to identify environmental conditions in which precautions against heat illness should be observed. This is the method adopted by the American College of Sports Medicine in their Position Stand on Prevention of Thermal Injuries During Distance Running (1984). When the WBGT is between 23° C and 28° C, the runners are advised that they are at high risk for heat injury. Moderate risk is defined as 18° − 23° C WBGT; low risk, below 18° WBGT. The document also recommends that consideration be given to cancelling or rescheduling a race if WBGT exceeds 28°.

Part of the difficulty in identifying a single CET or WBGT value that would apply to all athletes competing under the same environmental conditions is the shifty nature of the ULPZ. A number of factors can shift the ULPZ higher or lower on the CET/WBGT scale and many of them are under the control of the athlete.

ACCLIMATIZATION / ACCLIMATION

Adaptation to heat through acclimatization to the natural environment or acclimation to an artificial environment is probably the most effective factor in extending the prescriptive zone to a higher CET or WBGT. Lind (1970) suggests that the ULPZ could be increased by 2° CET for acclimatized males while other investigators (Kuhlemeier, Miller, Dukes-Dobos, & Jensen, 1977; Wyndham, Strydom, Morrison, Williams, Bredell, Maritz, & Munro, 1965) found that the difference in the ULPZ depended on the metabolic rate. At low levels of exercise, the effect of acclimatization ($\sim$ 0.1° CET) was less than at high metabolic rates ($\sim$ 0.6° CET). No matter what the absolute improvement in the ULPZ may be, acclimatization does improve the athlete's ability to tolerate prolonged exercise in hot environments. Sweating begins at a lower Tc, and the amount of sweat produced per unit rise in internal temperature is increased (Nadel, Pandolf, Roberts, & Stolwijk, 1974).

This increase in the sensitivity and capacity of the sweating system permits the acclimatized athlete to dissipate more heat earlier during exercise, reduces $\overline{T}_{sk}$, and decreases the rate of increase in Tc. Since the acclimatized athlete also has a lower basal Tc (Givoni & Goldman, 1973), tolerance time in the heat is prolonged because it takes longer for Tc to reach a critical level (Baum, Bruck, & Schwennicke, 1976) When thermal equilibrium can be attained, the steady state Tc will be lower at a given exercise intensity following acclimatization. In turn, the decrease in core temperature reduces the demand on the circulatory system, decreasing exercise heart rate by as much as 20-40 bpm (Eichna, Park, Nelson, Horvath, & Palmes, 1950; Gisolfi, 1973).

For an endurance athlete, competing at an intensity and in an environment which does not permit thermal equilibrium, decreasing the rate at which Tc rises may mean the difference between completing the race or being forced to drop out. To extend the limits of performance in a hot environment, the athlete must plan ahead. The optimal acclimatization protocol would be to train in an environment comparable to that in which the competition is to be held—hot-dry conditions for the Tuscon marathon and warm-humid conditions for the Honolulu marathon—gradually increasing intensity and duration until able to exercise comfortably at the planned race pace for at least 100 min. Simulating the competitive condition is necessary since acclimatization to a hot-dry environment does not guarantee protection in hot-wet conditions, and acclimatizing at 30% $\dot{V}O_2$ max will not be adequate protection when exercising at 70% $\dot{V}O_2$ max (Gisolfi, Wilson, & Claxton, 1977). When natural acclimatization is not feasible, the alternative is acclimation in a controlled environment or by providing a microenvironment by training in a warm-up suit which raises skin temperature but still permits some evaporation of sweat. Whatever technique is chosen, care must be taken to avoid excessive hyperthermia during the acclimation or acclimatization procedure.

Physical Training and Heat Tolerance

The endurance athlete whose daily training sessions elevate Tc and stimulate the sweating response has a distinct advantage over nonathletes when suddenly faced with the challenge of competing in a hot environment in the unacclimatized state. Although a great deal of controversy surrounded a report by Piwonka, Robinson, Gay, and Manalis (1965) that male distance runners responded to exercise in the heat as though they were fully acclimatized, further study has confirmed their belief that training in a cool environment does improve exercise-heat tolerance (Gisolfi & Cohen, 1979; Pandolf, 1979). When compared to nonacclimatized males exercising in the same hot environment, endurance athletes will have a lower Tc, lower HR, higher $\dot{m}_{sw}/\Delta Tc$, lower $\bar{T}_{sk}$, and longer tolerance times (Gisolfi, 1973; Nadel, Pandolf, Roberts, & Stolwijk, 1974). Similar results have been observed for female distance runners (Drinkwater, Kupprat, Denton, & Horvath, 1977).

The likelihood of physical training improving heat tolerance of untrained men is enhanced when training intensity exceeds 50% $\dot{V}O_2$ max, duration of training is 8 weeks or longer, and core temperature is elevated during exercise (Pandolf, 1979). Under these conditions, physical training can account for ~50% of the improvement in heat tolerance achieved in normal heat acclimation procedures. Cohen and Gisolfi (1982) reported a similar effect for women participating in a high intensity interval training program in a cool (22° C) environment for 11 weeks. After training, performance time in a heat tolerance test (45°/24° C; db/wb) increased while HR, Tc, and $\bar{T}_{sk}$ all decreased. Not surprisingly, when trained men and women are acclimated to heat by the usual laboratory procedures, they acclimate faster and more completely than untrained individuals (Cohen & Gisolfi, 1982; Piwonka & Robinson, 1967).

STATE OF HYDRATION

During prolonged strenuous exercise in the heat an athlete may lose 1.0 - 1.5 liters of body fluid per hour in sweat. If that loss is not replenished, the effectiveness of the thermoregulatory system will eventually be compromised. Heart rate and core temperature will rise, and $\dot{m}_{sw}$ at any given Tc will be diminished. In effect, the ULPZ will be shifted left narrowing the prescriptive zone. Hypohydration increases the risk for heat injury by reducing the transfer of heat from the core to the periphery (Nadel, Fortney, & Wenger, 1980). As internal temperature rises, the demand on the circulatory system may exceed its ability to supply an adequate blood flow to both the muscles and the cutaneous circulation. Since metabolic needs take precedence, skin blood flow is decreased, heat transfer restricted, and Tc rises rapidly (Nadel, Fortney, & Wagner, 1980).

It is not certain that hyperhydration is as effective in increasing the ULPZ as hypohydration is in decreasing it. However, both Tc and HR are lower than in the unhydrated state so some benefit is obtained from consuming extra fluids prior to exercising in the heat (Greenleaf & Castle, 1971; Nadel, Fortney, & Wenger, 1980).

ROLE OF PHYSICAL FITNESS

In 1960, Irama Åstrand pointed out that core temperature was more closely related to relative workload (% $\dot{V}O_2$ max) than to absolute workload. Yet the prescriptive zone, and more importantly the ULPZ, was determined by assigning the same workload or task to all subjects regardless of individual fitness levels. Lind (1970) did not consider the variability in response excessive, but it is obvious from his data that at any given CET core temperature could range as much as $\pm$ 0.6° C from the group mean. Since it has been observed that industrial workers pace their work so energy expenditure averages ~35% $\dot{V}O_2$ max and seldom exceeds 50% $\dot{V}O_2$ max, Drinkwater and Horvath (unpublished observations) designed a protocol in which subjects exercised at 30% and 50% $\dot{V}O_2$ max in environments representing a wide range of CET and WBGT values. Women were selected as subjects since all previous studies of the prescriptive zone had used men. The results were useful in answering two questions: Does expressing metabolic rate as a %$\dot{V}O_2$ max reduce variability in response? Can the concept of the prescriptive zone and ULPZ be applied to women as well as men?

The first question remains unanswered since previous studies did not report the standard error of estimate for the equilibrium line within the prescriptive zone. However, a 95% confidence interval of ± 0.56° C for the 30% $\dot{V}O_2$ max sessions was close to the range of scores observed by Lind (1970) for light work. The ULPZ for women exercising at 30% $\dot{V}O_2$ max was 29.4° C, almost identical to that calculated for men, 29.3° C. The ULPZ of 26.3° for unacclimatized women exercising at 50% $\dot{V}O_2$ max was slightly less than that (27.4° C) for acclimated men performing similar work. The difference is probably related to the acclimatization rather than to gender.

CONCLUSION

Heat injury is a potential threat to any athlete who trains or competes for long periods at high levels of intensity when environmental conditions inhibit heat dissipation. There are several ways in which athletes can improve their heat tolerance and thereby improve their performance. However, at present there is no way of identifying the precise combination of environmental conditions that place an individual athlete at risk in the heat.

REFERENCES

AMERICAN College of Sports Medicine. (1984). Position stand on prevention of thermal injuries during distance running. *Sports Medicine Bulletin,* **19**.

ÅSTRAND, I. (1960). Aerobic work capacity in men and women with special reference to age. *Acta Physiological Scandinavica,* **169**, Supplement, 1-92.

BAUM, E., Brück, K., & Schwennicke, H.P. (1976). Adaptive modifications in the thermoregulatory system of long-distance runners. *Journal of Applied Physiology,* **40**, 404-410.

BLIGH, J., & Johnson, K.G. (1973). Glossary of terms for thermal physiology. *Journal of Applied Physiology,* **35**, 941-961.

BUSKIRK, E.R. (1977). Temperature regulation with exercise. *Exercise Sport Science Reviews,* **5**, 45-88.

COHEN, J.S., & Gisolfi, C.V. (1982). Effects of interval training on work-heat tolerance of young women. *Medicine and Science in Sports and Exercise,* **14**, 46-52.

DRINKWATER, B.L., Kupprat, I.C., Denton, J.E., & Horvath, S.M. (1977). Heat tolerance of female distance runners. *Annals of the New York Academy of Science,* **301**, 777-792.

EICHNA, L.W., Park, C.R., Nelson, N., Horvath, S.M., & Palmes, E.D. (1950). Thermal regulation during acclimatization in a hot, dry (desert type) environment. *American Journal of Physiology,* **163**, 585-597.

GISOLFI, C. (1973). Work-heat tolerance derived from interval training. *Journal of Applied Physiology,* **35**, 349-354.

GISOLFI, C.V., & Cohen, J.S. (1979). Relationships among training, heat acclimation, and heat tolerance in men and women: The controversy revisited. *Medicine and Science in Sports,* **11**, 56-59.

GISOLFI, C.V., & Wenger, C.B. (1984). Temperature regulation during exercise: Old concepts, new ideas. *Exercise Sport Science Reviews,* **12**, 339-372.

GISOLFI, C., Wilson, N.C., & Claxton, B. (1977). Work-heat tolerance of distance runners. *Annals of the New York Academy of Science,* **301**, 139-150.

GIVONI, B., & Goldman, R.F. (1973). Predicting effects of heat acclimatization on heart rate and rectal temperature. *Journal of Applied Physiology,* **35**, 875-879.

GREENLEAF, J.E. (1979). Hyperthermia and exercise. In D. Robertshaw (Ed.), *International Review of Physiology. Vol. 20. Environmental Physiology III.* Baltimore: University Park Press.

GREENLEAF, J.E., & Castle, B.L. (1971). Exercise temperature regulation in man during hypohydration and hyperhydration. *Journal of Applied Physiology,* **30**, 847-853.

KERSLAKE, D. McK. (1972). *The stress of hot environments.* Cambridge, England: University Press.

KUHLEMEIER, K.V., Miller, J.M., Dukes-Dubos, F.N., & Jensen, R. (1977). Determinants of the prescriptive zone of industrial workers. *Journal of Applied Physiology: Respiratory, Environmental and Exercise Physiology,* **43**, 347-351.

LIND, A.R. (1963). A physiological criterion for setting thermal environmental limits for everyday work. *Journal of Applied Physiology,* **18**, 51-56.

LIND, A.R. (1970). Effect of individual variation on upper limit of prescriptive zone of climates. *Journal of Applied Physiology,* **28**, 57-62.

NADEL, E.R., Fortney, S.M., & Wenger, C.B. (1980). Effect of hydration state on circulatory and thermal regulations. *Journal of Applied Physiology: Respiratory, Environmental and Exercise Physiology,* **49**, 715-721.

NADEL, E.R., Pandolf, K.B., Roberts, M.F., & Stolwijk, J.A.J. (1974). Mechanisms of thermal acclimation to exercise and heat. *Journal Applied Physiology,* **37**, 515-520.

NIELSEN, M. (1970). Heat production and body temperature during rest and work. In J.D. Hardy, A.P. Gagge, & J.A.J. Stolwijk (Eds.), *Physiological and behavioral temperature regulation.* Springfield, IL: Thomas.

PANDOLF, K.B., (1979). Effects of physical training and cardiorespiratory physical fitness on exercise-heat tolerance: Recent observations. *Medicine and Science in Sports,* **11**, 60-65.

PIWONKA, R.W., & Robinson, S. (1967). Acclimatization of highly trained men to work in severe heat. *Journal of Applied Physiology, 22,* 9-12.

PIWONKA, R.W., Robinson, S., Gay, V.L., & Manalis, R.S. (1965). Preacclimatization of men to heat by training. *Journal of Applied Physiology, 20,* 379-384.

ROWELL, L.B. (1983). Cardiovascular adjustments to thermal stress. In J.T. Shepherd & F.M. Abboud (Eds.), *Handbook of Physiology.* Section 2. *Cardiovascular System.* Vol. 3. *Peripheral Circulation and Organ Blood Flow.* Bethesda, MD: American Physiological Society.

WYNDHAM, C.H., Strydom, N.B., Morrison, J.F., Williams, C.G., Bredell, G.A.G., Maritz, J.S., & Munro, A. (1965). Criteria for physiological limits for work in heat. *Journal of Applied Physiology, 20,* 37-45.

Factors Limiting Springboard Diving Performance: Historical and Biomechanical Perspectives

Doris I. Miller
University of Western Ontario

Progress in a sport such as springboard diving can best be judged by the increased difficulty of the dives being executed. The forward 1 1/2 that was common several decades ago has been replaced by the 3 1/2, and some men are now performing 4 1/2 somersaults in competition. Similarly, the number of twists incorporated into dives has increased to 3 1/2 or 4. What are the reasons for these improved performances? How much further can we expect the sport to go? In attempting to answer these two questions, the first from a historical and the second from a biomechanical perspective, I will restrict my comments primarily to the performances of United States male divers. Where possible, exemplary data from the analysis of Greg Louganis' dives at the 1983 US National Sports Festival will be provided because Louganis is considered by many to represent the pinnacle in springboard diving performance.

HISTORICAL PERSPECTIVE

In retrospect, we can appreciate how springboard diving has been influenced by better equipment and facilities as well as by changes in the rules and nature of the competition. Although not addressed here, superior technique and training methods have also played important roles in extending the horizons of the sport.

Equipment and Facilities

The springboard used in competition has undergone major changes over the years: in length (from 12 to 16 ft); in slope (from an 8 in. elevation gain to completely level); and in fulcrum design (from a rigid fulcrum to one that is readily adjustable). In addition, standards for water depth beneath the board have increased from a minimum of 7 ft to 12 ft under a 1 m board.

In terms of construction, the competitive springboard has evolved from wood to aluminum alloy. In 1922 (Sullivan, 1922), the official board for "fancy diving" had to be 12 to 13 ft long, at least 20 in. wide, and at least 2 ft 6 in. (but not more than 4 ft) above the surface of the water. The fulcrum, which was fixed, had to be located at least 33% of the board length from the free end. The suggested construction was "six 2-inch by 4-inch strips of straight grained white ash" covered with cocoa matting. By 1928 (Sullivan, 1928), the design had been refined by Stanford coach Ernst Brandsten. The so-called "Brandsten board," strongly recommended for intercollegiate competition, was 14 ft long, made of "selected vertical straight grain Oregon pine in one piece" and sloped upward 2 to 2.5 degrees. While the fulcrum (now 57% of the length from the free end) could be adjusted in a limited way, it was anything but freely movable.

In 1951, the NCAA rules no longer stipulated that the board had to be made of wood. This change was the result of the adoption of the multiunit aluminum "Buckboard" built by the Norman Buck Manufacturing Company of Seattle (Torney, 1959). The Buckboard was then used in major competitions for almost a decade, only to be supplanted in 1959 by the "Duraflex," a single unit aluminum alloy board tapered from fulcrum to tip. In 1969, the "Dura-maxi-flex" was developed by adding a second taper (from the fulcrum back). An improved version, the "Dura-maxi-flex B," which has perforations in the tip and was marketed in 1979, was used in the 1984 Olympic Games. According to the manufacturer (Arcadia Air Products), this board recoils faster and drains water from the tip more effectively than the preceding model.

Thus, today's competition springboard is no longer a fixed fulcrum, 12- to 14-ft heavy wooden plank covered with coconut matting. Modern diving boards are 16 ft long, made of aluminum alloy, tapered toward both ends, and mounted level. While the term "running dive" is still retained, the approach is more of a walk than the run previously necessitated to clear the end of the upward sloping board. The freely movable fulcrum can accommodate differences in strength and movement speed of various divers. Consequently, divers are able to depress the board considerably more. For example, Louganis, deflects the board about .9 m in dives with running approaches. It is this area of matching the diver's physical capabilities to fulcrum position that requires scientific investigation. At present, fulcrum setting is largely determined empirically on the basis of "feel" and experience.

Competition

To determine changes in the actual dives performed over the years, it would be ideal to have copies of the diving lists of Olympic and national finalists. Unfortunately these are difficult to obtain (if in fact anyone has preserved them). An alternate, although somewhat less satisfactory, approach is to examine the nature of the competition and the types of dives included in the rulebooks. The latter approach was undertaken to gain further insight into the improvement of diving performances. Primary reliance was placed on swimming handbooks from the NCAA (and its precursors) to obtain this information.

In 1922, men were required to perform four dives from the low (1 m) board: a running forward dive (plain or swallow); a back dive; a running forward jack-knife; and a back jack-knife (what we now term an inward dive pike). In addition, they had to do four others from a list of 23 optional dives. Included in this list was a flying Dutchman (also termed an Isander, a forward spring backdive, later a half gainer, and finally a reverse dive). At that time, handstand dives were executed from the then fairly stable springboard. The highest degree of difficulty (DD) of 2.2 was awarded for four different dives: a forward 1 1/2 with 1/2 twist; a back 1 1/2; a forward double;

and a forward jack-knife with a full twist. All entries were supposed to be made within 6 ft from the end of the board. To assist judges in assessing this distance, a mark was placed on the edge of the pool deck.

By 1931, a 3 m board was required for NCAA championships. In addition, the competition was defined as consisting of five compulsory and six voluntary dives. The compulsory dives were a running plain header forward; backward header standing; running Isander (half gainer); backward spring and forward dive; and a running header forward with a half screw. It is interesting to note that essentially the same dives have persisted as compulsories until the present in NCAA competition, as has the concept of five compulsories and six optionals.

Although the basic structure of the competition has changed little over the past half-century, the diving tables have gradually become longer as more and more difficult dives have been incorporated. In 1937, forward 3 1/2 and cut-away 2 1/2 (i.e., inward) somersaults were added with DDs of 2.5 (Kennedy, 1937). Already present in the tables were back and gainer (reverse) 2 1/2s also with DDs of 2.5. While other dives have been included over the years, it should be noted that the reverse 3 1/2 was added in 1981 (DD 3.2) and subsequently, in 1982, the forward 4 1/2 (DD 3.5); back 3 1/2 (DD 3.4); and inward 3 1/2 (DD 3.4). As of 1984, the NCAA rulebook listed some 76 different springboard dives (11 forward, 8 back, 8 reverse, 8 inward, and 41 twist).

It was not until 1982 that the nature of international springboard competition altered significantly. Prior to that time, with some minor alterations, divers had to perform five compulsory dives (i.e., forward dive; back dive; reverse dive; inward dive; and forward dive with a half twist). In addition, they had to do six optional dives including one from each of the five groups. In 1982, the international (FINA) rules changed so that the total DD for compulsory dives (one selected from each of the five groups) could not exceed 9.5. While this still forced competitors to do the simpler dives well, it allowed for greater variety as it did not limit them as narrowly as before. As a result, the 1 1/2 made a comeback. The remaining (optional or voluntary) dives had no DD limit. Therefore, this is the part of the competition in which quadruple somersaults and twists were seen.

BIOMECHANICAL PERSPECTIVE

In competition, the bulk of the judges' score rests upon the results of the diver's vertical and angular momentum during the flight. The average score is weighted by a DD factor with more credit being given to a greater number of somersaults and twists and to diving positions with a larger moment of inertia about the spinning axis. Success in the flight depends upon height or time in the air (related to vertical momentum) and upon the ability to perform multiple somersaults and twists with control and finesse (related to angular momentum).

Vertical Momentum

Height achieved in a springboard dive is directly related to the vertical momentum (and thus the vertical velocity) at the completion of the take-off. Consequently, to investigate factors limiting the height of the dive, we must examine what is occurring during the take-off.

In a recent study (Miller & Munro, 1984), we analyzed factors influencing the magnitude of the vertical velocity at the end of the take-off. Three were identified: the magnitude of the downward velocity at board contact following the hurdle; the upward acceleration of the diver relative to the board resulting in an active push downward against the board; and dissipation or absorption of force due to negative acceleration with respect to the board. The second factor would appear central to the present discussion.

During depression, the diver attempts to accelerate upward with respect to the board and thereby increase its downward deflection. Although all of the divers were able to do this to some degree, none could maintain that upward acceleration throughout board depression. Rather, the upward acceleration of the diver with respect to the board was limited to approximately the first half of that portion of the take-off. (Analysis of Louganis' running dives at the 1983 US National Sports Festival likewise revealed that he could only sustain this active push downward against the board for the initial 57 to 61% of springboard depression.) When the vertical acceleration was partitioned into the total (active and passive) contributions of the legs, trunk-head, and arms, it was evident that the legs accounted for about 75%, dominating the active push (Miller & Munro, 1984). Consequently, it appears that the major limitation to achieving maximum board depression is related to the ability to generate effective extensor torques with the lower extremity musculature.

In analyzing the performance of the simpler dives up to and in some cases including back, reverse, and inward 2 1/2s and the forward 3 1/2 for male competitors, it would seem logical to assume that further improvements will lie in increasing the board depression and thereby leading to greater height and more time in the air. In addition to the generation of effective extensor muscle torques of the lower extremities, springboard depression might be enhanced by better matching of the diver's physical capabilities with fulcrum position to maximize board depression.

Angular Momentum

If we are to examine potential limitations or areas of improvement for the most difficult dives (back, reverse, and inward 3 1/2s; forward 4 1/2; and triple and quadruple twists), then, in addition to height, we must examine the build-up of angular momentum during the take-off. Once the diver leaves the board, the only external force in fluencing the flight is the body weight acting downward through the center of gravity. Since the line of action of the weight passes through the center of gravity, the weight can have no moment of force or torque with respect to that point. Thus, whatever angular momentum with respect to the center of gravity is generated by the end of the take-off will remain unchanged in magnitude and direction throughout the flight.

To date, little attention has been directed to the generation of angular momentum and there is a particular need to focus on the role of the individual segments in this process. An interesting observation made by US diving coach Charlie Catuso could serve as a ''springboard'' for this kind of investigation. It has been recognized that the Chinese divers, who are among the best in the world, appear to spin extremely rapidly. One might speculate that their generally smaller statures and associated smaller moments of inertia might be contributing factors. However, Catuso noted a major alteration in their take-off technique which differentiates them from most other competitors. The difference seems to lie in the arm position at initial contact with the board following the hurdle. Whereas American divers tend to be completing the downswing of the arms when they land on the board, the Chinese are already beginning their upswing so that the hands are slightly ahead of the hips at board contact. This means that their arms, while sacrificing some of their contribution to actively depressing the board, can begin to generate angular momentum earlier and perhaps produce higher angular momentum magnitudes.

In the case of Louganis' 3 1/2 pike, the legs, arms, and trunk-head contributed almost equally to the total body angular momentum of 70 kg-m-m/s. Consequently, the arms assume a larger role in this aspect of the performance of multiple somersaulting dives than in the generation of vertical momentum for the flight. This topic deserves further investigation.

An answer to the question of how far we can yet expect the sport of diving to go would be purely speculative. Factors such as board construction, fulcrum position in relation to the physical capabilities of the divers, ability to generate large reaction forces with the legs, as well as the timing and speed of movement of the extremities and trunk, all play a role in determining if the sky is indeed the limit in springboard diving.

REFERENCES

KENNEDY, E.T. (Ed.). (1937). *National Collegiate Athletic Association official rules for swimming, fancy diving and water polo.* New York: American Sports Pub. Co.

MILLER, D.I., & Munro, C.F. (1984). Body segment contributions to height achieved during the flight of a springboard dive. *Medicine and Science in Sports and Exercise,* **16,** 234-242.

SULLIVAN, F.J. (Ed.) (1922). *Intercollegiate swimming guide.* New York: American Sports Pub. Co.

SULLIVAN, F.J. (Ed.) (1928). *Intercollegiate swimming guide.* New York: American Sports Pub. Co.

TORNEY, J.A. (Ed.) (1959). *The official National Collegiate Athletic Association swimming guide.* New York: The National Collegiate Athletic Bureau.

Morphological Factors Limiting Human Performance

J.E. Lindsay Carter
San Diego State University

Writers, artists, scientists, and lay persons across the centuries have recorded characteristics of physique that they have associated with success in different human performances and sports. But what is so empirically obvious has not been so easy to quantify, and little has been done to directly relate these characteristics of physique in theoretical and experimental studies with performance. It is the intent of this paper to examine morphological factors that are related to, and that may limit, human physical performance. The discussion will be limited to consideration of macroscopic factors that can be determined by external anthropometry and associated techniques. Physiological and biomechanical aspects that are related to morphology are purposely left to others.

Morphology is the science of structure and form without regard to function, but it is a basic biological dictum that form follows function, and so there is a relationship between the two. For as D'Arcy Thompson has so eloquently stated, "Morphology is not only a study of material things, but has its dynamical aspect, under which we deal with the interpretation, in terms of force, of the operations of Energy." (Thompson, 1966, p. 14). He points out that matter as such produces nothing, changes nothing, and does nothing, yet cells can never act as matter alone, but only as seats of energy and as centers of force. Thus morphology, or physique, is related to the physiology and biomechanics of the human body in motion. Masses, levers, and forces are the cornerstones of human movement, and their quantification is the foundation for building a more complete knowledge of human performance.

Which characteristics of physique are important for success in different types of performance? The nature and level of performance are likely to influence the characteristics and degree of association expected. With reference to Olympic levels of performance, Tanner (1964) observed that lack of the proper physique may make it almost impossible for an athlete to reach that degree of success. In general, the most productive studies have been of high-level performers at national and international levels. Theoretically, we would expect those who are most successful to have the appropriate structures commensurate with their performance task; therefore, examination of differences between these structures and tasks will increase our understanding of the importance of aspects of physique.

HISTORICAL PRECEDENTS

Measurement of the morphology of athletes has largely developed during the past century. Studies during this time have focused on descriptions of athletes, comparisons of athletes between and within sports, relationships of physique to physiology and biomechanics, and selection of young athletes for training. In their review of physique and sport performance, or "sport anthropometry," Tittel and Wutscherk (1972) cited more than 100 sources. Since then probably 100 more have been published. With regard to studies on Olympic athletes, 14 major books or monographs have been published, the earliest by Knoll (1928) and the latest by Carter (1984). A comprehensive review of these studies has recently been made by Borms and Hebbelinck (1984).

In the United States, Sargent (1887) made extensive anthropometric and functional tests on large numbers of Harvard University students and athletes. He noted that development of athletes was "governed largely by the constitutional bias of the individual, the sport in which he is engaged, and the time devoted to it." (p. 541). Although his athletes were not of today's caliber, he demonstrated certain physical characteristics in them that are quite similar to findings 100 years later.

ANTHROPOMETRIC-BIOMECHANICAL MODELS

If there is a common criticism of many of the studies cited above, it is that they have been largely descriptive, with only a few containing substantive statistical comparisons. Direct experimental work relating structure to top-level performance is difficult (if not impossible) without interfering with the development of the athlete. Because of this it appears that biomechanical modeling of physique changes and performance will be more appropriate, and that future training will attempt to match the model.

There are few theoretical models developed for testing the contributions of physique to performance. Two models, by Tittel (1978) and by Hay and Reid (1982), provide a rationale for relating physique and performance. Both have some characteristics in common. They identify masses, lengths, and forces as integral parts of their "box-diagrams" for explaining performance. Tittel describes active and "ballast" tissues acting in force-lever, and force-load relationships, and notes that these can be estimated by anthropometric methods. Hay's models are deterministic in that consecutive levels of the models are completely determined by mechanical factors in the lower level. For example, in the qualitative analysis model for the high jump, takeoff height is determined by two factors—physique and position. Physique is represented by the lengths, masses, and location of centers of gravity of the athletes' body segments. The positions of the segments—their lengths and angles—also help determine takeoff height. These factors are amenable to anthropometric measurement.

Furthermore, in the complete model for the high jump (Figure 1), physique and position of body parts are factors in clearance height (and may affect the style used), and vertical forces and mass are factors in producing change in vertical velocity of the jumper. Thus segment lengths, tissue masses, and muscular forces (estimated from corrected girths) are factors of physique that have anthropometric equivalents, and in-

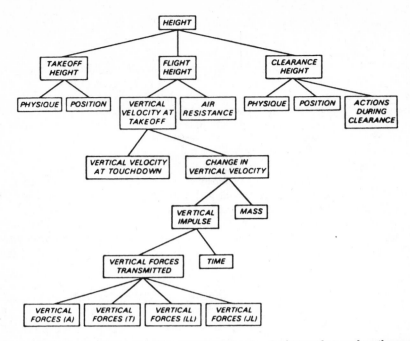

Figure 1—Biomechanical model of the high jump showing the factors that produce the result (i.e., height jumped). Factors that can be measured by anthropometry are physique, position, mass, and forces (through muscle size and lever lengths). (From Hay & Reid, 1982)

formation on these factors may provide better understanding of contributions of physique to high jump performance. If the physiology and biomechanics of the tissues involved in human performance are to be fully understood, then quantification of the anatomical structures is paramount.

Human performance is a multivariate phenomenon. In addition to physique, such factors as physiological function, biomechanical constraints, psychological state, environment, and sociocultural context all may affect performance. Knowledge of the variation (or lack of it) in physique can provide us with useful parameters through which we can relate other factors affecting performance. However, in some studies so little information is given about the physical characteristics of the subjects as to render the findings of negligible value when one considers the variety of the human species.

A relatively new and comprehensive approach to assessment of physique is through kinanthropometry, which evaluates the physical structure of individuals in relation to gross motor performance. The term *kinanthropometry* is derived from morphometry, which is the measurement of shape and form, and anthropometry, which is the measurement of shape and form of man. Kinanthropometry is the quantitative study of size, shape, proportion, composition, and maturation in relation to gross motor function (Figure 2). As examples, the kinanthropometric approach has been successfully used to study the physical structure of Olympic athletes (Carter, 1982, 1984), national teams in different sports (Perez, 1981), and as part of a national athlete-testing program (Ross & Marfell-Jones, 1983).

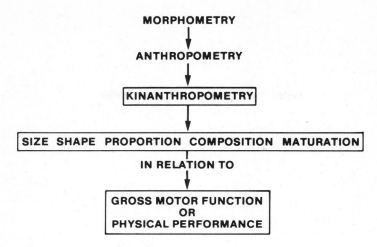

Figure 2—Derivation and content of kinanthropometry.

PHYSIQUE AND PERFORMANCE

Because of the almost infinite variety of physical characteristics and performance tasks, only a summary is possible of present knowledge of morphological factors limiting human performance. In addition, some examples of recent findings will be given, with most taken from studies of elite athletes. The presentation will follow the areas of study within kinanthropometry.

Absolute Body Size

There is overwhelming evidence showing differences in body size between athletes in different sports, whether measured by weight, height, lengths, breadths, girths, or skinfolds—between sports or within sports by event. Syntheses of this information for Olympic athletes from 1928 to 1976 are contained in Carter (1984), and for age, height, and weight for athletes at recent Olympics in Hirata (1979). Although there are clear differences in some comparisons, there is considerable overlap in dimensions between athletes in some sports and events. Moreover, athletes from different sports range from very small to very large (Carter, 1978).

When absolute height or weight are related to success in an event, we would expect people with the appropriate size to be more successful than others without these characteristics. For example, when mean heights and weights for athletes in track and field events at the Montreal Olympics were compared by gender, there was a typical gender dimorphic pattern regardless of event (Carter, 1984). These differences were similar in magnitude to those in normal populations. However, in addition to this biological difference, there were differences in height and weight across events that were common to both males and females. This indicates that these changes in absolute height and weight are related to the biomechanical or physiological demands of the events. Although we might expect less influence of height or weight on performance

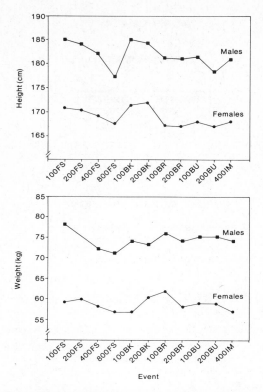

Figure 3—Sexual dimorphism in height and weight of male and female Olympic swimmers at Montreal by event. (Adapted from Hirata, 1979).

in swimming compared to track and field events, similar differences by gender and event are observed as shown in Figure 3.

When many size variables are available on a sample or an individual, comparisons against profiles of all athletes are useful. In these profiles the variables are scaled to centiles or z-scores in order to show the characteristics of athletes in different events, or to show how an individual differs from the average of athletes in their chosen event (Carter, Ross, Aubry, Hebbelinck, & Borms, 1982).

Body weight is a limiting factor in strength. This relationship has been examined in Olympic weight lifters by Ross and Ward (1984) and Sale and Norman (1983). Weight lifted increases with weight class, but larger lifters are relatively weaker. Relative strength increases with mass to the 0.69 power, which is very close to the theoretical expectancy of mass to the 0.67 power, if we assume shape and composition to be geometrically similar by weight class.

Shape

Several methods of measuring shape or form of the body have been applied to the study of athletes, and one of these is that of somatotyping (Heath & Carter, 1967; Carter,

1980). Somatotyping has been used to describe differences in athletes from different sports by Carter (1981, 1984), De Garay, Levine, and Carter (1974), Perez (1981), Štěpnička (1977), and Tanner (1964).

Extensive studies of the somatotypes of athletes at different levels of performance have shown that there are limitations in somatotype characteristics of athletes in different sports and events. However, as with body size, some athletes with the same somatotypes are successful in different events. These differences have been shown at different levels of competition and are often present in young athletes (Carter, 1978, 1981; Perez 1981).

An example of the differences in somatotype by event and gender in track and field is given in Figure 4. Mean somatotypes for different events are plotted, and the shaded areas represent the 95% limits of the somatotype distributions of athletes in all events (Carter, 1984). The means for both genders have a fairly consistent pattern of increasing endomorphy and mesomorphy, with decreasing ectomorphy, from distance runners to shot-discus-hammer throwers for males, and from jumpers to shot-discus throwers for females. There is a consistent pattern of sexual dimorphism which is very similar for each event, and the differences between events indicate that different somatotypes are required for success at this level of competition.

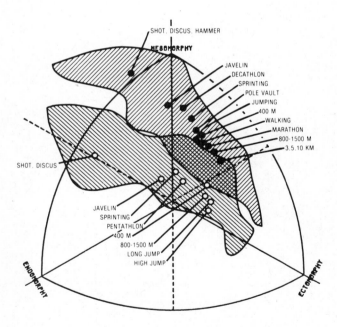

Figure 4—Somatochart showing mean somatoplots for male (above) and female (below) Olympic track and field athletes by event. Data from the Mexico City and Montreal Olympics were combined for plotting. Shaded areas include 95% of all somatotypes for each sex. (From Carter, 1984).

PROPORTIONAL BODY SIZE

Although absolute size is important in many events, proportional size may be more relevant in other events. For example, in weight lifting it is theoretically desirable to have relatively short levers for force application. In general, weight lifters do have short levers and these are proportional to the size of the lifter. Furthermore, distance runners show little variation in proportional mass, but they can differ widely in absolute height and weight.

The proportionality approach of Ross and Wilson (1974) has been most useful in making comparisons between athletes in different sports and events, and between genders in the same event (Ross, Ward, Leahy, & Day, 1982; Ross & Ward, 1984). Essentially, the approach is to mathematically adjust all persons to the same "phantom" height and express deviations from scaled values in terms of z-scores based on a unisex reference phantom. This allows for comparisons to be made between sexes, at different ages, and between different sports, against the same reference scale. Using this procedure, Ross and Ward (1984) examined secular trend in male Olympic track and field event groups from 1928 to 1976. They showed that proportional weight has increased dramatically in shot-discus-hammer throwers since 1960, and also in javelin

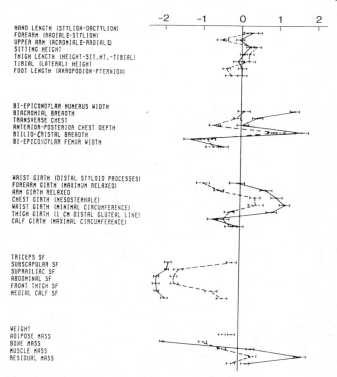

Figure 5—Proportionality profiles of z-values for male (solid lines) and female swimmers (broken lines) from the 1976 Olympics. Horizontal bars represent means +7- one standard error. (Redrawn from Ross et al., 1982)

throwers since 1968. Athletes in other events were proportionally lighter, and no clear secular trend was noted except for a gradual increase in sprinters.

A proportional analysis, using a wide variety of anthropometric measures taken on male and female swimmers at the 1976 Olympics, is shown in Figure 5. As inferred from the nonoverlap between the horizontal standard error bars, male swimmers are proportionally longer in forearm, tibia, and foot length, larger in all breadths except femur breadth, and smaller in biiliocristal breadth than female swimmers. In addition, males are smaller in skinfolds and adipose mass, but larger than females in the other three fractional masses (see body composition). Both sexes are close in relative weight.

In addition to analysis of the Montreal Olympic data, Ross and Ward (1984) have reanalyzed data from the Rome and Mexico City Olympics. They confirm and amplify the proportional differences in athletes in different events, as well as ethnic differences within events. For example, black athletes tend to have proportionally longer arms, legs, shorter trunk, and narrower hips than white athletes. They also noted that compared to males, female athletes appear to have a persistent upper-lower body musculoskeletal dysplasia and a limb-torso skinfold dysplasia.

BODY COMPOSITION

Body composition in athletes is a topic of great interest and controversy. Athletes in many sports are concerned with shedding excess weight that may diminish optimal performance, and sport scientists have attempted to make "best estimates" of body fat as the most expendable "ballast." However, the simple truth is that most methods provide only rough estimates of a single tissue or fluid and assume constants for the other tissues or fluids in the multi-compartmented body. The evidence is all in the direction of considerable variation in the masses and densities of all disectable compartments of the human body (Martin, 1984). Little progress will be made in body composition assessment until we can quantify more accurately, allowing for individual variation not only regarding fat but also bone, muscle-tendon, connective tissue, and other anatomical or chemically defined compartments for the whole body. This knowledge is important if we are to relate in a meaningful way gross structure to biomechanical and physiological variables.

On the other hand, empirical evidence and common sense show that many athletes have extremely low levels of fat however it may be estimated. When fatness is low in athletes, there is little variation among those in the same event at high levels of competition; therefore, larger variation is in fat-free weight, which in many cases is very close to body weight.

Of practical importance to many athletes is identification of the lowest levels of skinfolds compatible with optimal performance and health. Based on skinfolds at six sites on 2,000 Olympic athletes, Carter and Yuhasz (1984) proposed a "critical region" of skinfold values which would encompass acceptable low levels. Examples of these regions for male and female athletes have been constructed and are shown in Figure 6. The width of each region is sufficient to allow for ethnic and individual patterns of skinfolds, as well as measurer and instrument error. The low boundaries are the lowest skinfolds for each site measured on Olympic athletes; the high boundaries are

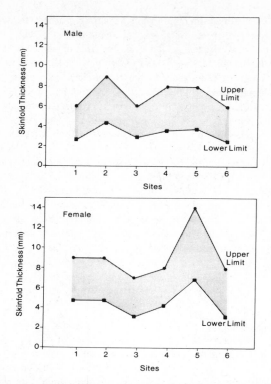

Figure 6—"Critical region" for lowest skinfold thickness in Olympic male and female athletes. Sites 1-6 are triceps, subscapular, supraspinale, umbilical, front thigh, and medial calf, respectively.

essentially double the rounded low value. Monitoring of skinfolds of athletes can serve to indicate how close the athlete approaches minimal acceptable levels of total fatness.

An anthropometric method of providing estimates of masses for fat, bone, muscle, and remainder has been proposed by Drinkwater and Ross (1980), and used in the study of athletes (Hebbelinck, Ross, Carter, & Borms, 1980; Ross et al., 1982). Both absolute and proportional masses can be calculated by this promising approach from simple anthropometry (see Figure 5).

MATURATION

Anthropometry of growing children is traditional for monitoring normal and abnormal growth. With the increased emphasis in youth sports in many countries, and the precocity of some athletes in such sports as female gymnastics and swimming, questions arise regarding the effects of training on growth and maturation.

Recent articles have reviewed some of the questions (Malina, Little, Bouchard, Carter, Hughes, Kunze, & Ahmed, 1984; Märker, 1981; Ross & Marfell-Jones, 1983). In general, elite male and female swimmers are normal or slightly advanced in maturation, but female gymnasts, track distance runners, figure skaters, and divers are delayed. These latter sports require the girls to move their body mass against gravity, and a high strength-to-mass ratio would seem to be advantageous. The mechanisms of the delayed maturation are not clear, but longitudinal data by Märker (1981) show no detrimental effects on reproductive functions and childbearing. Furthermore, young athletes seem to grow in a similar manner to, but at a different rate than, reference children, their physiques being generally consistent with those of older athletes in the same sport or event (Malina et al., 1984).

CONCLUDING REMARKS

Absolute and relative size, somatotype, composition, and maturation are morphological factors that may limit human performance. It is inferred that athletes who have, or acquire, the optimal physique for an event are more likely to succeed than those who lack these characteristics. Quantification of physique through kinanthropometry can provide a better basis for understanding the limits related to biomechanics and physiology of performance.

REFERENCES

BORMS, J. & Hebbelinck, M. (1984). Review of studies of Olympic athletes. In J.E.L. Carter (Ed.). *Physical structure of Olympic athletes, Part II: Kinanthropometry of Olympic athletes.* Basel: Karger.

CARTER, J.E.L. (1978). Prediction of outstanding athletic ability: The structural perspective. In F. Landry & W. Orban (Eds.), *Exercise Physiology (Vol. 4).* Miami: Symposia Specialists.

CARTER, J.E.L. (1980). *The Heath-Carter somatotype method.* San Diego: San Diego State University Press.

CARTER, J.E.L. (1981). Somatotypes of female athletes. In J. Borms, M. Hebbelinck, & A. Venerando (Eds.), *The female athlete.* Basel: Karger.

CARTER, J.E.L. (Ed.). (1982). *Physical structure of Olympic athletes, Part I: The Montreal Olympic Games anthropological project.* Basel: Karger.

CARTER, J.E.L. (Ed.). (1984). *Physical structure of Olympic athletes, Part II: Kinanthropometry of Olympic athletes.* Basel: Karger.

CARTER, J.E.L., Ross, W.D., Aubry, S.P., Hebbelinck, M., & Borms, J. (1982). Anthropometry of Montreal Olympic athletes. In J.E.L. Carter (Ed.), *Physical structure of Olympic athletes, Part I: The Montreal Olympic Games anthropological project. Basel: Karger.*

CARTER, J.E.L., & Yuhasz, M.S. (1984). Skinfolds and body composition of Olympic athletes. In J.E.L. Carter (Ed.), *Physical structure of Olympic athletes, Part II: Kinanthropometry of Olympic athletes.* Basel: Karger.

DE GARAY, A.L., Levine, L., & Carter, J.E.L. (Eds.). (1974). *Genetic and anthropological studies of Olympic athletes.* New York: Academic Press.

DRINKWATER, D.T., & Ross, W.D. (1980). Anthropometric fractionation of body mass. In M. Ostyn, G. Beunen, & J. Simons (Eds.), *Kinanthropometry II*. Baltimore: University Park Press.

HAY, J.G., & Reid, J.G. (1982). *The anatomical and mechanical bases of human motion*. Englewood Cliffs, NJ: Prentice-Hall.

HEATH, B.H., & Carter, J.E.L. (1967). A modified somatotype method. *American Journal of Physical Anthropology, 27*, 57-74.

HEBBELINCK, M., Ross, W.D., Carter, J.E.L., & Borms, J. (1980). Anthropometric characteristics of female Olympic rowers. *Canadian Journal of Applied Sports Science, 5*, 255-262.

HIRATA, K.I. (1979). *Selection of Olympic champions, Vols. I-II*. Toyota: Chukyo University.

KNOLL, W. (1928). *Die sportarztlichen Ergebnisse der II. Olympischen Winerspiele in St. Mortitz*. Bern: Haupt.

MALINA, R.M., Little, B.B., Bouchard, C., Carter, J.E.L., Hughes, P.C.R., Kunze, D., & Ahmed, L. (1984). Growth status of Olympic athletes less than 18 years of age. In J.E.L. Carter (Ed.), *Physical structure of Olympic athletes, Part II: Kinanthropometry of Olympic athletes*. Basel: Karger.

MÄRKER, K. (1981). Influence of athletic training in the maturity process of girls. In J. Borms, M. Hebbelinck, & A. Venerando (Eds.), *The female athlete*. Basel: Karger.

MARTIN, A.D. (1984). Quantification of skin, adipose tissue, muscle, and bone in adults: Evidence from cadaver dissections and a critique of some in vivo methods. Unpublished doctoral dissertation, Simon Fraser University.

PEREZ, B. (1981). *Los atletas venezolanos. Su tipo fisico*. Caracas: Universidad Central de Venezuela.

ROSS, W.D., & Marfell-Jones, M.J. (1983). Kinanthropometry. In J.D. MacDougall, H.A. Wenger, & H.J. Green (Eds.), *Physiological testing of the elite athlete*. Ottawa: Canadian Association of Sport Sciences.

ROSS, W.D., & Ward, R. (1984). Proportionality of Olympic athletes. In J.E.L. Carter (Ed.), *Physical structure of Olympic athletes, Part II: Kinanthropometry of Olympic athletes*. Basel: Karger.

ROSS, W.D., Ward, R., Leahy, R.M., & Day, J.A.P. (1982). Proportionality of Montreal athletes. In J.E.L. Carter (Ed.), *Physical structure of Olympic athletes, Part I: The Montreal Olympic Games anthropological project*. Basel: Karger.

ROSS, W.D., & Wilson, N.C. (1974). A strategem for proportional growth assessment, In J. Borms & M. Hebbelinck (Eds.), *Children and exercise. Acta Paediatrica Belgica, 28*, Supplement, 169-182.

SALE, D.G., & Norman, R.W. (1983). Testing strength and power. In J.D. MacDougall, H.A. Wenger, & H.J. Green (Eds.), *Physiological testing of the elite athlete*. Ottawa: Canadian Association of Sport Sciences.

SARGENT, D.A. (1887). The physical characteristics of the athlete. *Scribners,* **2,** 541-561.

ŠTĚPNIČKA, J. (1977). Somatotypes of Czechoslovak athletes. In O.G. Eiben (Ed.), *Growth and development: Physique.* Budapest: Akademiai Kiado.

TANNER, J.M. (1964). *The physique of the Olympic athlete.* London: Allen & Unwin.

THOMPSON, D.W. (1966). *On growth and form.* (Abridged edition by J.T. Bonner). Cambridge: Cambridge University Press.

TITTEL, K. (1978). Tasks and tendencies of sport anthropometry's development. In F. Landry & W. Orban (Eds.), *Biomechanics of sports and kinanthropometry, Vol. 6.* Miami: Symposia Specialists.

TITTLE, K., & Wutscherk. H. (1972). *Sportanthropometrie.* Leipzig: Barth.

Philosophical Considerations in Human Performance

Hans Lenk
Universität Karlsruhe

When Bob Beamon did his winning 8.90 meter jump at the 1968 Olympic Games, many newspapers hailed it as a leap into the next athletic millennium. Scientists, too, considered it "most probably a limit of athletic capability" there being "no other world track or field record that excels the previous best performance by a comparable margin . . . Beamon's feat outshines all others. It is unlikely that the 8.90 meter record will ever be beaten." I quote Ernst Jokl (1977). With Carl Lewis, the apparently impossible has become possible, indeed likely, again.

Are there any absolute limitations in Olympic sport? It is a fact that in view of the constant output of records in more than one branch of sport, the question arises as to whether Olympic top-performance sport has become the exclusive prey of record mania. Is an end of the record series at all possible, and does a statistical survey give us any indication of the future quantitative and qualitative development of records?

To begin with, it is not right to assert that top-performance sport is to be seen under the absolute domination of the record; most of the Olympic sports do not permit records, and it is only in six or so of the almost 30 official Olympic sports that official record lists are kept. Even in the record-oriented events, athletes capable of breaking a world record at the Games value the Olympic victory much higher than the record as such. A record might be established elsewhere, or under more favorable conditions, but it is only here and now—at the Olympic Games—that a competitor can score an Olympic victory: *"Hic Olympia, hic salta!"*

Nor is it right to claim, as many critics do, that as a human being the athlete is totally eclipsed by his or her record in its numerical manifestation. Records established by Paavo Nurmi or Emil Zatopek are forgotten and have been rendered obsolete long since (even these men, exceptional runners in their day, would today find themselves lapped) but have the names and images of these sporting personalities disappeared? Sporting performances must be seen against the background of history—of their time and of the social circumstances. They cannot be separated from the persons involved; they cannot be dealt with in isolation or simply in quantitative abstraction. Anyone who reduces the pursuit of excellence in competitive sport to mere record figures and the enumeration of medals has fallen victim to a one-sided approach, the distorted perspective that is encouraged by certain exaggerations of the media.

Admittedly, there have also been Olympic authors, such as Pierre de Coubertin (1966) and Carl Diem (1942, 1949), and philosophers such as José Ortega y Gasset

(1930), and lately, Paul Weiss (1971), who have taken the stance that sporting records bear a relation to natural laws. The records indicate, in terms of a constant and ever closer approach to the limits of human achievement, what humans are capable of as performing beings. De Coubertin believed that sporting activity was crowned by records just as Newton's axioms were the climax of physics. Diem and Weiss considered that records were a manifestation of natural laws, that Kant's question, "What is Man?" would be answered in exemplary form by the top-performance athlete and his or her record. Admittedly in each case it would be a temporary answer provocative of challenge, but nevertheless an indefatigable movement toward the limits of human performance, a continual exploitation of the reserves of improvement available before these limits are reached. Let us check and elaborate this Kantian question and relate it to the problems of human performance.

The human race cannot be captured in just one definition or formula. Its essence cannot be characterized by just delineating one trait. Any philosophical definition or theory of the human race has to take into account many perspectives; no theory can be monolithic. Philosophers have tried to define humankind by an outstanding definition or feature as, for example, "rationality." Aristotle defined man as the rational animal or, in addition, as the social being. Modern philosophers have tried to characterize the human as the working being (Marx, 1962; Marx & Engles, 1959), as the being who is dependent on developing instruments, the tool-making being (Franklin, 1962), as the symbolic being (Cassirer, 1956; Langer, 1957). Existential philosophers have mainly emphasized the faculties of freedom and decision making. Authors in philosophic anthropology proper, such as Plessner (1975), used to stress the eccentricity, the faculty of self-distancing, and "the functional transcendence" (Keller, 1974) of man compensating for the biological lack of an encompassing natural instinctive outfit and biological determination.

The human therefore is dependent on self-made flexibility and variability, supplementation, self-perfection, and all kinds of cultural institutions. Gehlen (1940) would even call culture the human being's second nature. Within this framework he tried to define man as the acting being (i.e., the being who is not only moving and behaving, but acting in a fashion oriented at goals it intentionally strives for). The German philosopher Odo Marquard (1983) tried to define man as the compensating being, that is, the being who is necessarily obliged to cope with insufficiencies and dissatisfactions as well as all kinds of shortcomings and sufferings by compensating mechanisms, institutions, and coping actions.

In short, philosophers have tried to interpret humankind by allegedly unique faculties using some fine and proper Latin names as, for example, *homo faber, homo cogitans, homo agens, homo loquens, homo ludens, homo laborans, homo creator* and, recently, *homo compensator.* Most notable for physical education and sports was Huizinga's definition of man as *homo ludens.*

However, all these definitional features were certainly not able to encompass all phenomena of human life and aspirations. Any monolithic theory of humankind and monodefinitional effort seems to fail because no specific trait by itself would suffice to capture the specific humanity of man (woman). As we know, no necessary condition would do for a definition, nor would a conjunction or disjunction of a few necessary features. Necessary conditions are not by themselves sufficient conditions. A definition or full-fledged criterion must capture the necessary as well as the sufficient conditions. Therefore, a realistic philosophic anthropology is to be multifactorial or pluralistic. It has to go beyond a single factor approach. Nietzsche's (1906) ambiguous description of man as the being not yet ascertained and not yet determined seems to be still valid today.

Keeping this in mind, we might nevertheless reflect on some intriguing and very important central features, as for instance the characterization of the human as the acting being (by Schütz, 1971, and Gehlen, 1940) as mentioned above.

I think that the characterization of man (woman) as the acting being is still too general. The human is not only characterized by goal-oriented behavior and the consciousness and intentionality in trying to achieve goals; this would be true of other primates also. I rather believe that man (woman) seems to be more specifically characterized as the being who is able to materialize goals better in the striving for and achieving them. More than any other primate, the human is able to assess own actions by using standards, by comparing them with the actions of others in a rational and objective way. Achieving does imply acting, however. Therefore, the more intriguing feature that philosophical anthropologists and phenomenologists such as Gehlen (1940) and Schütz (1971) had in mind might be considered as this capability of rational, systematic, and objective improvement of one's actions leading to a special refinement of action patterns as well as levels. And therefore the human seems to be the personally acting and performing being at the same time—the personally achieving being.

Personal proper achievement, accomplishment, and performance seem to be very important and ideal traits of a full-fledged human being as a cultural being. Proper personal action and achievement are among the most specific designating traits of humankind. This is certainly true if we interpret achievement in its widest sense in which any personal engaging actions meeting certain levels of quality or standards are involved. It is all the more valid if we take "achievement" in the narrowest sense of the term as an ever improving measurable accomplishment or performance, particularly in competition.

Concerning higher aspirations, the human is not just acting on a minimal level or just trying to compensate. Rather, he or she acts in a specific way using some criteria of rationality, economy, improvement, facilitation, and creativity. The "achieving being" certainly implies more than merely the acting being or the compensating being. One does not try just to make good for shortcomings and sufferings, but to take them as challenges in order to be able to overcompensate, to act in a creative, noncompulsive manner. It is not just passive compensation that is decisive here, but active creative improvement according to standards. Man (woman) therefore is *homo actor, homo performator,* and *homo creator* at the same time. Proper and personal achievement is a very important, necessary trait within the pluralistic spectrum of defining traits for humankind.

If we take personal and proper action as a criterion of real life in a deep anthropological and even existential sense, we might say that only he or she who acts, achieves, and improves something and the self can be called alive. Genuine human life in the deepest sense seems to be personal achievement, engagement, and performance in the mentioned sense. This is true at least in Western culture and in all active cultures if we take "achievement" in its narrowest sense. It might be considered valid in any culture whatsoever, too, if we take "achievement" in its wider sense mentioned above.

This insight certainly and easily applies also to the realm of physical education, bodily movement, sports, and athletics. I would even say that in sports we find a realm of life in which genuine personal achievement is still to be encountered everywhere, notwithstanding any attempt of institutionalization, delegation, administration, and so forth. In sport, achievements and actions cannot be vicariously achieved, delegated, pretended, or obtained surreptitiously: Sport involvement necessarily is personal; it requires a real personal endeavor and effort and a genuine proper action, at times even total personal devotion.

"Concern for bodily excellence"—a slogan Paul Weiss (1971) so aptly phrased for featuring athletics—is also concern for personal achievement and involvement. If active and creative life in its deepest sense is proper and personal action, active sporting activity can be considered a paradigmatic instantiation, a vehicle and medium for this kind of active life. Sport in a world of institutions and their administrative grip has been able to remain an oasis of genuine active personal involvement, of genuine life, so to speak. In this sense, we can even accept the inference of the Spanish philosopher of life, Ortega y Gasset (1950), that sport is genuine life, though we might not support his inverse conclusion that all life in its deepest sense would be sport; this would mean an extreme extension of the concept of sport beyond any sensible identifiability. There are indeed other areas of creative life and achievement beyond sports.

Since it is only man (woman) who can properly achieve as a person, and since free will and self-motivation are necessary conditions of any creative personal involvement, sport is not just a natural phenomenon but at the same time it is a psychophysical and sociocultural phenomenon of symbolic character. This is also reflected in the world of sport in diverse forms. The multiplicity of patterns of movements and their variations and modalities are vehicles of the plurality and diversity of world orientations and personal experiences in sport. Multiplicity of movement is an expression of cultural, and at times personal, differentiation. Marcel Mauss (1978) has impressively described in cultural, historic, and phenomenological studies how different movement patterns and different cultures obtain. Not only the nature of movement and its natural variation, but also cultural impregnation, the "culture" of movement, so to speak, is an intriguing field for anthropologists of sport. This is true not only for everyday movements but to a certain degree also for folk sports and for the cultural descendance of many an international sport.

In performance sport we are confronted not just with everyday motor development, but rather with highly schematized, standardized, rationalized, and systematized processes and developments. Sport movements do obey special controls and conventions. However, within the scope of constitutive rules and norms, personal proper variants, modifications, and new discoveries and developments may obtain. Think of Fosbury's flop or very difficult new exercises in gymnastics. It is only by precise comparison that objective judgments, assessments, and improvements are possible. Only conventionalization, regulation, and precise monitoring allows for the considerable plurality of different sport disciplines and forms of movements within these. By such means the movements of sports got, and would at times still get, a new meaning and significance. This is true even for running and walking as athletic disciplines that seem rather stylized and artificial as compared with everyday movements.

Sport movements are a part of a special social institution, of a symbolic *eigen-*world within the world. But this is only true on an analytical level of interpretation. For sports at the same time are real actions in the normal world, though artificially impregnated. They are artifacts with a meaning of their own. By learning and mastering difficult sport movements, athletes orient themselves within the world and explore this world as well as their own body and the respective relationship between both of them by using new variants of expression, orientation, and self-confirmation.

This can be easily illustrated by difficult movements that require months of exercise before being fully mastered. Frequent failures in the seemingly impossible attempt to extend one's limits and even the automatization of movement coordinations in training show the same phenomenon: If you do not master the movement (e.g., a Yamashita jump with a full turn or even a somersault) you will necessarily have to prepare it by many exercises, each under conscious self-control and concomitant monitoring as well as analytical decomposition. In the beginning, help and support is required. The movement will be badly performed at first, just approximately completed or awkwardly performed. The body is experienced as being something clumsy and resistant which has to be pressed into a very raw form of the successful movement. An ideal image of the completed and successful jump is the goal and standard of orientation, but it seems to be depressingly far away.

Within a series of many raw premovements and supported attempts, all of a sudden the athlete performs a successful jump. The first experience "to have done it" and the first impression of successfully mastering the challenge loom. Later the athlete succeeds more frequently. A ban seems to be broken. Help and support become superfluous. The extreme concentration of consciousness may gradually be reduced in the wake of an ever improving automatization of coordination and by external as well as kinesthetic and proprioceptive control. This opens resources of concentration for other external tasks such as variants, modifications, refined corrections, and strategic considerations. The movement is now a part of the repertory of the mastered exercise.

All movements of sport seem to be learned and achieved like that. The succession of the learning phases is obvious particularly with difficult and risky movements. On higher levels, respective phases of the learning process are repeated. If coordination of movements is no longer a problem, consciousness turns to overriding strategies.

The same is also true for sport actions and movements with equipment requiring a similar series of phases of raw framing and coordinative automatization. Metaphorically speaking, equipment such as the tennis racket or the rower's oar or the downhiller's ski can be described as a quasi elongated part of one's own arms or legs, which tie in with the interplay of perceptions of resistance and feedback of success and failure, as well as with the learning phases. In addition to the normal kinesthetic experiences and processes of fatigue, the clumsiness of the equipment must also be perceived, controlled, and overcome in a series of instances of the movement. Being able to master the equipment certainly depends on the varying quality and form of the equipment, as well as on situations of the environment. The coping with objects as obstacles stands out much more here than, for instance, in running, which is a relatively "natural" movement that nearly everybody is able to perform.

Generally speaking, sporting movements in a wider sense are active proper achievements, results of a systematic and goal oriented self-discipline, of a specific learning process. They may admit within the framework of given patterns, rules, and norms of personal modifications, optimizations, variants of style, and so forth. The plurality of rules impregnating sport movements indeed differentiates the possibilities of movement behavior, and thereby also of personal expression, of the personality which might be considered as a dynamical structure of actions and dispositions as well as psychic impulses and habits. Psychophysically speaking, sporting actions require an encompassing involvement of the person. They are real and genuine proper actions and achievements. Though in a way conventionalized and standardized, top-level sport performances require such a personal involvement and devotion to exercise, training, and personal self-development that they cannot be commanded. You can compel somebody to march but not to establish a world record in the marathon or to win a gold medal in gymnastics' all around competition.

Sport movements in part extend one's natural motor capacities, but beyond that they are conventionalized, standardized, and impregnated by idealized patterns and images that are cultural, historical, and social in origin. Sport movements are, so to speak, artificial, determined by artificial obstacles or deviations. One would literally choose superfluous obstacles (i.e., hurdles) and prescribe complicated patterns and rules in order to overcome these obstacles in a most elegant, effective, or efficient manner. Sport sets up artificial obstacles in order to prove perfection by the overcoming of these obstacles—or at least by approximating perfection in the process. A kind of relativized self-perfection via a symbolic expression seems to be achieved only by systematic preparatory training for a long time. Top-level achievement in sport is a symbolic, artificial cultivation of psychophysical personal involvement under the challenging idea of social comparisons or in comparison with one's previous level of performance.

A personal proper achievement (Eigenleistung) in sport—and in particular a top-level performance—can and should be considered a creative expression of personality. In that sense, sport might be considered one variant of the liberal arts—the eighth art, so to speak, within the spectrum of the traditional seven fine arts—even though the product or work is not material but symbolic. Therefore, sports might be interpreted as a performing art of a specific kind, with a special emphasis on personal activity. The active part seems to be more important here than the passive spectator sport, even though top-level achievements seem to generate a special fascination for onlookers, too.

Extraordinary achievements in sport cannot come as a result of drill, dressage, or orders. An athlete must voluntarily accept the challenge. Without some large margin of personal freedom, no genuine achievement or real personal involvement or autonomous personal development seems possible. You cannot just command somebody to creatively achieve at top-level in any realm. Therefore, achievement in sport and in any other creative activity remains an expression of personal freedom. Even though many social, political, or other manipulations may be relatively important, personal identification and personal action still play the most important role here.

On the other hand, achievement in the sporting performance is not just an individual phenomenon, since it is impregnated by socially established patterns, norms, and rules. It is only possible within an institution. Competitive sport at least is dominated by the so-called achievement principle, which seems to be a social abstraction according to which one's achievement status is assessed only within the hierarchy of competing participants. In sport, an almost pure utopian construction of achievement norms can be found that is hardly encountered in such a pure form elsewhere, not even in the world of labor. The sporting achievement principle may be looked upon as representing a kind of pure essence of achievement behavior. Its standardization and value depend on symbolic interpretation and instrumentation rendering possible strict measurement, visibility, comparability, and simple understanding. On the other hand, this abstraction is not carried to such an extreme that one would lose sight of the similarities, analogies, and correlations of this rather artificially stylized behavior-model to the corresponding ones in everyday life. This might also be true for the motivations.

Performance in sport is usually considered to be but an instance of achievement motivation covered by McClelland's (1961) and Atkinson's (1958) theory of achievement motivation, which is supplemented by Weiner's (1972) more recent theory of causal attribution. While this might be true in general, there are typical deviations from the overall motivational pattern of these theories, particularly for top-level risk sports. Only in the last decade have some psychologists (i.e., Zuckerman, 1979) paid attention to the rather deviant patterns of motivation found in top-level mountaineers, surfers, car racers, parachuters, and others.

In other, more normal sports as well, a newly termed motivation of high sensation seeking might combine with other traditional motivations. Zuckerman (1979), for instance, distinguishes "high sensation seekers" from "low sensation seekers." High sensation seekers really do search for risks, adventures, and new experiences. Usually the correlations with traditional values on the n-achievement scales of motivation theory are negative because, according to Atkinson (1958) and McClelland (1961), highly achievement motivated persons are rather searching for tasks of medium- rather than high-risk challenges. High sensation seekers seem to differ from traditional highly achievement motivated persons. Concerning high risks in the achievement behavior, as opposed to compulsory effort and endurance (Blankstein, Darte, & Donaldson, 1976), statistically significant positive correlations were found with the normal sort of achievement motivation.

It might be interesting for a psychologist to distinguish between several different types of achievement motivation. There are those who are highly risk-oriented, who seek extraordinary risk in their achievement actions (think of the solo mountaineer Reinhold Messner). Whereas the highly achievement-motivated subjects, according to Atkinson's (1958) and McClelland's (1961) traditional theory, prefer a medium level of difficulty and risks, the high sensation seekers would seek the challenge of the extreme. Athletes of risky sports such as mountaineering or scuba diving may be high personal-risk achievers. Neither plain risk orientation nor traditional achievement orientation by themselves seem to characterize such high risk achievers; rather, it seems that both factors together are necessary for creative productivity and risky achievements. This seems true for the so-called risk sports, but perhaps also for any strenuous top-level sport in which the seemingly impossible defines the limits that pose the challenge to put them further.

Top-level performances typically combine with new experiences or even experiences of high risk and limits. The traditional model of achievement motivation theory certainly had its difficulties with explaining risky achievements of superoptimal stimulation. More than a medium level of difficulty, tension, and risk seem to be instrumental in top-performance sport. Psychologists should research such a combination type reflected in high performance sport. In summary, then, it might be stated that proper personal achievement is an important category of philosophical anthropology that may be necessary in understanding sport action, particularly high-level performance. The human cannot be understood in his or her highly achieving aspirations if defined simply as "the acting being" without any more specific differentiation. Only if understood as "the personally achieving being" capable of proper personal involvement in setting, realizing and materializing his or her own goals better and better—though in a socioculturally impregnated framework—can the human being's high performances in any creative realm of activity be adequately interpreted.

This is particularly true for sport, too. Though sport does not lead to a materialized object as the result of the activity, it might be considered analogously as a kind of symbolic performing art which—though also fascinating for spectators—carries its meaning mainly for the performer. Top-level athletics might be considered a kind of high performance competitive dance.[1]

Clearly, the attempt to characterize the human as "the personally achieving being" refers to a necessary condition which only in combination with other traits might be considered a part of a sufficient characterization. In addition, philosophical anthropology cannot identify the problems of humankind by just definitional and descriptive efforts; it must develop a whole conceptual theory including normative aspects. The human being reflects his or her role and self-understanding in the framework of goals and objectives that he or she postulates and feels that he/she *should* live up to. In that sense, man (woman) is the normative and moral being, too. This means that philosophical anthropology cannot just stay with a descriptive account of overt behavior or a passive adaptation to constant social norms. Rather, man (woman) is also in that normative sense the active being depending on a dynamic interplay between relatively constant cultural institutional norms and an active interpretation, reconstruction, and further development of these. He or she is even dependent on defining and searching for challenges in order to realize and actively materialize a part of this dynamic essence.

In that sense the human is the challenge-seeking, risk-seeking being, keen on "pushing further the limits," as Ortega y Gasset (1950) would write. What shall we say about Ortega y Gasset's stance, which held that dynamic living generally, and its prototype, sport, in particular, was characterized by "an unruly urge to advance one's boundary stones"? Also, de Coubertin's Olympic maxim *"Citius, altius, fortius"*—a borrowing from Father Didon—would seem in the final analysis to presuppose a constant process of linear improvement as well as total record worship. It has been described by Willi Daume (1976) as "a most dangerous dictum" which, if treated with absolute validity, would amount to rather inhumane consequences.

If sporting performances are based on natural biological processes, they are nevertheless not determined or characterized by these alone. They are always motivated by cultural components and are dependent on conventions. For instance, the world javelin record cannot be regarded as the limit of human capability solely on the basis of natural laws, since the Basque javelin technique, which was prohibited by the International Amateur Athletic Federation, permits much longer throws. Conventional restrictions, cultural traditions, and even mythical situations and challenges to the human being which, though based on his or her status in nature, are nevertheless manifestations of cultural encounter of intrinsic or superimposed social forms. These help to determine a sporting performance, a sporting record, and possible limits of sporting capability. Thus, it is not the workings of natural laws alone, but a cultural image of symbolic import— and under the impulsion of the conflict with nature—that is the determining factor in sport, of its performances and limitations.

A sporting performance reproduces the symbolic dramatization of basic situations and the active struggle for mastery on the part of a goal-oriented human with his or

---

[1] I will not delve into the problems of the competition principle in sport here. Competition is indeed outstanding in Western sports, but there are also other ways of sport not directly oriented toward competition. Compare the Eastern Zen tradition in some sports, even in the seemingly highly competitive martial arts. Think also of some nature sports in which the symbolic opponent is not human but perhaps a glacier wall or an apparently insurmountable rock.

her orientation toward the comparison and improvement of performances. In sport we also find mythical elements. They are embodied in the simple actuation of partisanship, and in confrontation with an opponent or with nature, displaying a positively archetypal dramatic force and fascination, a readily perceptible and comprehensible dramatic build-up and action content (cf. Lenk, 1972, 1979). However, mythical elements invariably display cultural features. Ultimately, sport is not pure nature but a cultural phenomenon: the cultural canalization, modification, and representation of natural processes. Thus, statements about records and limits in sport cannot have a purely scientific basis or relevance, but they have a philosophic-anthropological and cultural significance.

Even de Coubertin (1966) had not enunciated his slogan *"Citius, altius, fortius"* in terms of absolute validity, averse though he was to all moderation, to all "excessive reserve," seeing in the "untrammelled exercise of sport its attraction . . . its justification . . . the secret of its moral values." The essential restriction on the apparently uncurbed "Citius, altius, fortius" ideal in de Coubertin's conception is of an ethical character. For de Coubertin there can be no sense in a record, a contest, a victory "at any price." To be "good," a performance is to be achieved by all means with the utmost effort, but only honestly and by permissible means. Fraud, manipulation, and all devices aiming at an unfair or artificial advantage, from the ethical standpoint, are anathema.

Furthermore, his Olympic motto cannot be interpreted as permitting fatal accidents or total incapacitation in Olympic sports. The ancient Greek *pankration,* an all-out contest leading to total disablement, would not have been in line with de Coubertin (1966) and his Olympic maxim. Tragic deaths, such as that of the Danish cyclist Jensen in Rome in 1960 and of the downhill skier Milne and bobman Skrypecki at Innsbruck in 1964, occurred outside the range of de Coubertin's axiom. Risks can be assessed only in general terms and reduced only to an approximate extent; they cannot be eliminated altogether, especially in the top performance range.

However, it is legitimate to ask whether some risks are escalated beyond the human limit, a hypertrophy of performance boosting into the realm of inhumanity that is sometimes countenanced, or even provoked, by international sport authorities. Must downhill courses be more dangerous and faster than all previous ones? Must there be a fatal accident before the worst perils are eliminated? We may be sure it is the pathos of mistaken heroism when anyone follows the example of some of the sporting world's existentialist philosophers in hailing precisely the fascination of such potentially lethal sports as mountaineering, car and motorcycle racing, or surfing, and chooses the very danger of death, the existential "courting of annihilation" as the basis for an existential analysis of sport. An individual case of death in sport, or of an injury with irremediable effects, would be a tragic negation of de Coubertin's fundamental idea.

Restrictions and limitations on sporting achievements must be assessed in varying contexts: a clear distinction must be made between the biological limits of achievement inherent in nature and the normative limits based on cultural canons, ethical criteria, and social conventions. It is not only the physiological, anatomical, and other medically ascertainable performance-curbing factors (i.e., premises inherent in nature) that are relevant for sporting achievement, and not only those imposed by social and cultural conventions, but also limitations based on ideas of humanity, natural behavior, and ethical considerations that must govern humane sport according to all valid concepts of the latter.

Genuinely marginal situations in the existential sense, risks to life and all demands on human emergency reserves therein involved are not justifiable—in terms of the idea of humane sport—as the normal practice of competitive sport, even in its extreme manifestations. Fear of death would naturally unleash greatly increased reserves of achievement and effect a much closer approach to hypothetical performance limits. It is precisely in order to prevent the risk of total exhaustion, the possible exploitation of the last emergency reserves of strength, that the ban against amphetamines, steroids, and similar drugs is fully justified ethically. The justification of such a ban lies not only in the desirability of fair and equal chances—equal doping being theoretically possible—but also in the general need to avert the risk of extreme self-inflicted damage.

It would be expecting too much of the athletes themselves to require them to erect and defend a mental barrier against the escalation of risks. An Olympic hammer thrower and gold medalist, Harold Connolly (private communication) once stated that before a crucially important contest a top-performance athlete was in a psychological state which made him inclined to take anything promising an improved performance "provided it was not actually lethal." Indeed, it is increasingly difficult to draw the line between the harmless, acceptable enlistment of medicine for the manipulation of achievements in top-performance sport and its dangerous manifestations. Here it is evidently necessary to have safety margins and more stringent regulations than those now in operation. The problem, perhaps an insoluble one, is unfortunately that of encompassing practicable and effective controls.

The problematic element is aggravated especially by the fact that the dynamics of constant performance-escalation are subject to a law of marginal utility, to a logistic curve. Constantly diminishing improvements at the summit require an ever increasing effort in terms of training and talent, as well as scientific, technical, sport-instructional, and psychological guidance; what ensues is a typical struggle for marginal advantages. A marginalist theory of the growth of records would, as in economics, provide a more encompassing and differentiated view than just summarizing statistics. In other words, athletes are required—even for only modest margins of improvement—to submit to ever increasing risks of overstrain, accidents, or potentially irremediable physical sacrifice in order to score a tiny margin of improvement in the top performance bracket. We must not forget the human basis of sport. For pedagogical and ethical reasons, a human sense of moderation must not be neglected in view of the fascination exerted by top performances and the eclipse of all existing records.

The limits of humanity naturally cannot in any precise sense be demarcated quantitatively, but there is nevertheless a need for prescriptive criteria and enforceable guidelines. The point at which sport ceases to be sport cannot be fixed in terms of natural laws; it is a matter of ethical assessments on the basis of the stated ideas of humanity, natural conduct, moral canons, and reasonable standards—all notions of cultural and historical origin—factors subject to change around an unchangeable nucleus. However, a serious code of sporting ethics which does not exhaust itself in superficial, nonbinding generalities has hardly yet reached even a rudimentary stage of development. Even when confronted with the mythical fascination of a unique and unsurpassable performance, sport must not forget the human element. The limitations of humanity are more restrictive than the artificially manipulable limits of physiology. And it is the limitations by the requirements of humanity that should receive priority, even though it cannot be determined in any degree of precision.

In a deep sense, performance, particularly top-level performance in sport, does reflect this challenge-seeking nature of man (woman) as an active being. Top-level athletes in that sense are trying to explore and symbolically to conquer frontier realms of life. In that sense sport is carrying important opportunities for the human risk and adventure motive. In extreme cases and fields of activities we might even trace high sensation seekers in top-level sport. Generally speaking, motivational processes and motives as interpretational constructs characterizing top athletes could be covered by a new combination type of motivation: The high risk and challenge-seeking motive in combination with a high need for achievement (cf. Atkinson, 1958; McClelland, 1961). It would be a rather intriguing task for social psychologists to study this combination type of motivation, since the traditional theory of achievement motivation seems to be rather unsuccessful in explaining very high achievement orientation and risky behavior in top-level sports. We cannot only look for an average level of risk taking in order to understand top-level achievement consequently reaching at and even beyond apparent human limits.

However, not only do psychologists and social psychologists have much yet to study about human performance, but so do philosophers. The philosophy of top-level achievement actions and motivation is still in its infancy. To date there is no really encompassing philosophy of achievement, particularly top-level achievement. Such a philosophical interpretation certainly must take into account biological as well as historical, cultural, and social factors. It would render an intriguing topic for a truly interdisciplinary investigation. Top-level sport might be considered an outstanding paradigm case for such an interdisciplinary endeavor. This is one main reason why sport offers such an interesting topic for a philosophy of humankind.

REFERENCES

ATKINSON, J.W. (Ed.) (1958). *Motives and fantasy in action and society.* Princeton: University Press.

BLANKSTEIN, K.R., Darte, E., & Donaldson, P. (1976). A further correlation of sensation seeking: Achieving tendency. *Perceptual and Motor Skills, 42,* 1251-1255.

CASSIRER, E. (1956). *An essay on man.* New Haven: Yale University Press.

DAUME, W. (1976). In *Süddeutsche Zeitung,* 27th/28th March.

DE COUBERTIN, P. (1966). *The Olympic idea.* Schorndorf near Stuttgart: Hofmann.

DIEM, C. (1942). Philosophie der Leibesübungen. In C. Diem, *Olympische Flamme.* Vol. 1, Berlin.

DIEM, C. (1949). *Wesen and Lehre des Sports.* Berlin, Frankfurt: Limpert.

FRANKLIN, B. (1962). Quotation by K. Marx. In *Marx-Engels, Werke 23.* Berlin: Dietz, p. 194.

GEHLEN, A. (1940). *Der Mensch.* Bonn: Athenäum, 1958.

JOKL, E. (1977). Zwei Weltrekorde. In H. Lenk (Ed.), *Handlungsmuster Leistungssport.* Schorndorf near Stuttgart: Hofmann.

KELLER, W. (1974). Philosophische Anthropologie—Psychologie—Transzendenz. In H.-G. Gadamer & P. Vogler (Eds.), *Neue Anthropologie*. Vol. 6. Stuttgart, München: Thieme.

LANGER, S.K. (1957). *Philosophy in a new key.* Cambridge: Harvard University Press.

LENK, H. (1972). *Leistungssport—Ideologie oder Mythos?* Stuttgart: Kohlhammer.

LENK, H. (1979). *Social philosophy of athletics. A pluralistic and practice-oriented philosophical analysis of top-level amateur sport.* Champaign, IL: Stipes.

LENK, H. (1983a). *Eigenleistung.* Zurich-Osnabrück: Interfrom.

LENK, H. (1983b). The achieving being and athletics. In H. Lenk (Ed.), *Topical problems of sport philosophy—Aktuelle Probleme der Sportphilosophie.* Schorndorf near Stuttgart: Hofmann.

LENK, H. (1984). Die achta Kunst. Zurich-Osnabrück: Interfrom.

MARQUARD, O. (1983). Homo compensator: Zur anthropologischen Karriere eines metaphysischen Begriffs. In G. Frey & J. Zelger (Eds.), *Der Mensch und die Wissenschaften vom Menschen.* Vol. 1. Innsbruck: Solaris.

MARX, K. (1962). *Das Kapital. Marx-Engels, Werke 23.* Berlin-East: Dietz.

MARX, K., & Engels, F. (1959). *Die deutsche Ideologie. Marx-Engels, Werke 3.* Berlin-East: Dietz.

MAUSS, M. (1978). *Soziologie und Anthropologie.* Vol. 2. Frankfurt, Berlin, Wien: Ullstein.

MCCLELLAND, D.C. (1961). *The achieving society.* Princeton.

NIETZSCHE, F. (1906). *Jenseits von Gut und Böse.* Werke Band VIII. Leipzig: Naumann.

ORTEGA Y GASSET, J. (1950). El origen deportivo des estado (1930). In *Obras completas.* Madrid.

PLESSNER, H. (1928). *Die Stufen des Organischen und der Mensch.* Berlin, New York: de Gruyter, 1975.

SCHÜTZ, A. (1971). *The problem of social reality. Collected papers I.* The Hague: Martinus Nijhoff.

WEINER, B. (1972). *Theories of motivation. From mechanism to cognition.* Chicago.

WEISS, P. (1969). *Sport—A philosophic inquiry.* Carbondale - Edwardsville: Southern Illinois University Press.

ZUCKERMAN, M. (1979). *Sensation-Seeking.* Hillsdale, N.J.: Erlbaum.

Limits to Human Performance—
The View From Space

Harold Sandler
Biomedical Research Division, NASA

Victor A. Convertino
University of Arizona

The harsh and demanding frontier of space was opened to humankind with the successful flight of Sputnik I in 1957 which marked the beginning of the Space Age. Within 4 years, man himself was launched into this new environment as first Yuri Gagarin and then John Glenn flew in orbit. The Space Age since then has seen men placed on the moon, cosmonauts inhabiting and working in a space station for 237 days, and development of a reusable space vehicle, the Space Shuttle. Present plans for completing permanent space stations before the turn of the century will require humans from many walks of life, females as well as males, to spend longer and longer periods in space. In this environment they will be faced with the stresses of weightlessness, inactivity, and confinement.

Much ground-based research, using primarily horizontal and head-down bed rest and immersion as simulators of weightlessness, has been conducted to determine the limits to mankind's well-being and performance in space. Such studies have provided considerable information on physiological limits of humans in space, and much of this information is applicable to activity on earth.

THE IMPACT OF GRAVITY

Gravity is a consistent factor governing life on earth. As humans, we spend two-thirds of our day normally in the upright or seated positions. In the upright position, a significant amount of intravascular volume and tissue fluid is shifted to the lower body because of the pull of gravity, and the body must compensate to maintain blood flow to the head and distribute the volume of blood adequately. When the compensatory mechanisms are inadequate or retarded, orthostatic intolerance or hypotension occurs with eventual fainting, or syncope.

Over time, the human body has evolved a gravity receptor system which uses the cardiovascular, neuroendocrine, and bone-muscle systems. It is controlled by muscle proprioreceptors, semicircular canals, otoliths, and mechanoreceptors (baroreceptors). These systems operate continually as we interact with our environment and its actions are most apparent when changing from the supine to erect body positions. This change shifts 700 ml of blood from the upper body to the legs, with 400 ml coming from the central circulation (heart and lungs). The loss in central blood volume immediately causes a 25% decrease in cardiac output, a 25% increase in heart rate, and a 40% decrease in stroke volume, with little change or even a slight increase in blood pressure. Blood pressure is maintained by an increase in flow resistance resulting from a sympathetic nervous system response. The process is reversed when changing from the erect to supine. Normally, 70% of the body's blood volume resides in the systemic veins, 15% in the heart and lungs, 10% in the systemic arteries, and 5% in the capillaries.

LEVELS OF DEFENSE IN BODILY POSITION CHANGES

At least three levels of defense offset cardiovascular changes that occur with changes in body position. The first is an adjustment in venous capacity and pressure by redistributing volume. When erect, venous volume is shifted primarily to the deep intra- and intermuscular leg veins, with about 200 ml going to the pelvis and gluteus maximus. Venous volume and pressure can be adjusted very rapidly by contraction and relaxation of smooth muscle in the venous wall, by respiration, and by contraction of limb muscles.

The second line of defense occurs when the pre- and postcapillary sphincters act to increase or decrease fluid in the tissues. Within 10 minutes of standing, about 10% of plasma volume is lost to dependent tissue spaces and this stabilizes at about 15% after 20 minutes. This second line of defense is probably more important in the long run than capacitance vessel shifts because it increases or decreases the volume of the cardiovascular system without redistributing its contents. Through such means absolute volume within the circulation can then be influenced greatly by factors at the local tissue level, ranging from nervous, metabolic, or biochemical events.

Finally, there is a third line of defense which is under neurohumoral control and used primarily for long-term adjustments. Responses can be measured during changes in environmental temperature or altitude, exercise or certain disease conditions such as diabetes insipidus, or inappropriate secretion of the antidiuretic hormone. Studies to date suggest that this third means of controlling blood volume is the one used by the body for long-term adaptation of the circulation to gravitational changes.

Activation of neurohumoral control depends on stimulation of proprioreceptors (baroreceptors) which, depending on whether they are located inside or outside the chest, and on their design, are able to sense: (a) the filling of the system, (b) the wall tension in atria or ventricles, or both, and (c) the pulse and mean pressures in the pulmonary and systemic arteries. When activated, the system stimulates sympathetic nerve activity, or inhibits release of potent hormone regulators, such as ADH. Long-term excitation of baroreceptors also changes the secretion of adrenal hormones (e.g., aldosterone) and the concentration of pressor substances (e.g., renin-angiotensin) from the kidneys. Recently, it has been suggested that ADH through regulating total circulating plasma volume may play a role in hypertension and the maintenance of proper blood pressure. It has also been clearly shown that atrial distention may release a natriuretic factor that controls loss of sodium and other electrolytes by the kidneys.

THE GAUER-HENRY REFLEX

The Gauer-Henry reflex hypothesis, which has long been accepted, claimed that distention of atrial receptors (mechanoreceptors) resulting from increased central blood volume, as going from erect to a supine body position, signals the central nervous system through the vagus nerve that there is excessive fluid present and results in ADH suppression. The result is a subsequent loss of fluid by the kidney, or a diuresis. This work was based on data from dogs, where vagus nerve section prevented diuresis in the majority of animals. However, recent work in nonhuman primates casts doubts on such explanation, since vagotomy has had no effect in preventing the diuresis caused by head-out water immersion (Gilmore, 1983). Such findings suggest that atrial stretch receptors are far less sensitive in primates, and probably in humans, and lead to the conclusion that high pressure baroreceptors, rather than atrial receptors, are responsible for control of urinary responses to heart distention in these cases.

That this may occur in the human has recently been shown by our own tests at Stanford University during tilt and water immersion studies of heart and heart-lung transplant recipients (Convertino and co-workers, 1983). These subjects, who have no nerve connections to the heart, should have failed to show plasma volume, plasma renin activity (PRA), and antidiuretic hormone (ADH) responses exhibited by normally innervated individuals, who have an intact vagus nerve—but they did. This area is presently under intense investigation. It carries high significance since regulation of body fluid and electrolyte contents is one of the chief physiologic challenges presented by flight in space or change in activity state on earth.

THE VIEW FROM SPACE

Space flight is still an experiment and will continue to be so for many years to come. Results indicate it is possible to survive weightlessness, but as we enter this next phase of the space program involving space communities, questions arise concerning the human's long-term presence in space and his or her ability to interact with the highly complex technological systems required for maintaining health while there. At present we have little information about long-term human presence; only a few people have been exposed to prolonged weightlessness so far. In the 23 years of manned space flight, just over 140 astronauts and cosmonauts (four of them women) have actually flown in space. The duration of exposure for 120 of these individuals has been less than 2 weeks. Only nine people (all Russians) have ever lived in space for 6 months or longer, with three cosmonauts setting the recent endurance record of 237 days on October 2, 1984. Information about these longer flights indicate ability to survive, but data concerning cosmonaut rehabilitation shows a long and slow period of recovery. Up to the present, the history of manned flights has been marked by concerns for safety, survival, and endurance. Under these conditions it has not often been possible to make critical physiological measurements. These remain to be done in the upcoming decade.

In weightlessness, the body assumes a semicrouching or fetal position (Nicogossian & Parker, 1982). The legs are used primarily to perch, with the feet secured in foot restraints or wedged into a convenient crevice to hold the body in place. When the legs are used at all, it is to propel the body to another location and the force is brief and infrequent, requiring only a minute fraction of the force required to move on earth. The arms are used mainly, and the force required to move them is similar to that required on earth.

Within a few hours into flight, blood shifts from the legs and lower back to the upper body, causing fullness of the head and engorgement of the neck veins, which persist throughout the entire flight regardless of duration. The decrease in force and movement in the major muscle masses of the body results in muscle atrophy, significantly decreased myocardial demand, and secondary changes in the heart. Normal stresses are removed from the tendons, articular cartilage, bone, and supporting tissues, since many important neuromuscular reflexes and coordinate movements are never used in space. In effect, space flight, through its change in activity or environment, causes changes in all body physiological systems. Many have different time courses of adaptation or change.

Vestibular disturbances occur early in flight. Although none were reported in the Mercury and Gemini missions, they were prevalent in Apollo flights, Skylab, and Shuttle missions, and in almost all Soviet flights. These disturbances include postural illusions, sensations of rotation, dizziness, vertigo, and motion sickness. They occur primarily when the eyes are open and can result in loss of appetite, nausea, and vomiting. The condition, which affects 30 to 40% of crewmen, persists from 2 to 4 days and then disappears. Crewmen who have flown previously appear to be less affected. Research continues on the causes of and countermeasures for space sickness, because a considerable number of crewmen are affected during a period when the most complex mission operations must be performed. Crews have also shown slower changes in the bone and muscle, with moderate persistent losses of calcium, phosphorus, and nitrogen. Calcium losses in the 84-day Skylab flight, for example, amounted to 0.5% per month of total calcium and have continued unabated throughout all flights in which measurements have been made.

To prevent severe muscle atrophy, flight crews have used various forms of exercise in both the U.S. and Soviet programs (Thornton, 1981). In the early Gemini and Apollo programs, bungie cords were used. The Skylab and Soyuz/Salyut missions, with their much larger space vehicles, permitted more sophisticated equipment and greater use of in-flight exercise. Skylab crewmen used a bicycle ergometer and stationary treadmill and were monitored during exercise for heart rate, ECG, blood pressure, respiration, and oxygen and carbon dioxide responses. Soviet crewmen used similar equipment (Gazenko, Genin, & Yegorov, 1981). With regular in-flight exercises, crewmen reported an improved feeling of well-being and postflight showed less weight loss, less cardiovascular deconditioning, and smaller losses of exercise capacity. During the Soviet 175-, 185-, 211-, and 237-day flights, crews exercised regularly and vigorously for as long as 3 hours a day. They also wore special load (Penguin) suits during waking hours. These suits contained elastic cords which attached to the hands and feet to provide resistance, or load, during regular motions. It was hoped that these garments would help prevent the cardiovascular changes and bone calcium losses seen with all flights.

Following flight, all crewmen have shown unstable blood pressure and heart rate when stressed by orthostatic tests (stand test, 70° tilt, LBNP). These changes have been observed regardless of whether a flight lasted 7 days or 6 months (Gazenko, Genin, & Yegorov, 1981; Sandler, 1980). The etiology of these changes is not fully known, but is attributed to a loss of intravascular volume resulting from the body's compensating for the headward fluid shift, inactivity, and decrements in nervous system control mechanisms (baroreceptor sensitivity). Exercise capacity postflight also has decreased by up to 50%. The heavy use of in-flight exercise has improved but not remedied the observed deconditioning.

Ground-based studies simulating the weightless condition with both athletes and nonathletes as subjects have provided valuable information. Although fluid immersion and bed rest do not precisely duplicate weightlessness, they *do* result in headward fluid shifts and orthostatic intolerance following exposure. Bed rest has been used more extensively because of the limitations inherent in immersion, but both have been invaluable in simulating physiological changes from weightlessness exposure and in testing countermeasures. Long-term effects, of course, are more effectively reproduced with bed rest.

Lately, head-down bed rest has been used primarily because of reports by crewmen that this position during postflight testing resulted in responses of head fullness and awareness more similar to those experienced during space flight. The results of head-down bed rest studies have been similar to data obtained after space flight.

DIFFERENCES IN RESPONSE OF MEN AND WOMEN

In preparation for the Space Shuttle program which will allow participation of older and sedentary subjects, men and women ages 35 to 65 were studied for physiological changes after 10 days of strict bed rest (simulating 7- to 10-day Shuttle flights). Responses of three groups—35 to 45 years, 45 to 55 years, and 55 to 65 years—were observed for cardiovascular deconditioning. Age did not appear to be a factor in cardiovascular deconditioning following bed rest. For example, the older men lost only 8.4% of their $\dot{V}O_2$ max, while younger men showed a 9.3% reduction (Convertino and co-workers, 1982; DeBusk and co-workers, 1983).

Comparison of work capacity in men and women 45 to 55 years showed little reduction (-0.8%) in the men, but a small but significant (4.7%) loss in the women. Before and after bed rest, both were able to reach their maximal workloads, but the women could sustain it for a much shorter time, while the men showed no change in tolerance time. The larger decrease in muscle mass (lean body weight) in the women (-5.1%) compared with the men (-1.9%) may have contributed. Moreover, the efficiency of oxygen transport, transfer, and utilization by muscle tissue was slightly reduced in the women, but not in the men.

RESPONSES OF TRAINED
VERSUS NONTRAINED INDIVIDUALS

Exercise tolerance (max $\dot{V}O_2$) as measured by supine bicycle ergometry has been measured before and after horizontal bed rest in trained (runners, 15 miles per week) and untrained subjects. Active men lost 14% of $\dot{V}O_2$ max and active women 10% of $\dot{V}O_2$ max with bed rest, but sedentary subjects lost significantly less (1% and 5%, respectively). An unexpected finding was the longer requirement of athletic individuals (3-4 weeks) to return to pre-bed rest levels. This occurred both for $\dot{V}O_2$ max and measured heart size, as well as intravascular volume. The reasons are still being investigated.

It should be noted that endurance-trained athletes have greater resting plasma and blood volumes than their nonathletic counterparts. When blood volume had been compared in our laboratories, trained women are seen to have an average volume of 5.67 L versus 4.07 L in untrained women, and trained men 6.58 L versus 5.25 L in untrained men. Men trained for competitive sports show an even higher blood volume of 7.45 L. Age, at least through middle age, has had no effect on these findings.

Despite their greater circulating plasma and blood volumes, athletes have shown a far greater incidence of vasodepressor syncope during orthostatic stress after bed rest, or immersion, as compared with sedentary persons (Klein, Wegmann, & Kuklinski; 1977). Why this occurs is not entirely clear, but may result from bodily adaptations during training. Water immersion studies have provided some insight into the causes. After head-out water immersion, untrained subjects have generally shown a 10% decrease in aerobic work capacity, while trained subjects have shown a 20% decrease.

Skipka and Schramm (1982) in Germany showed that plasma volume and diuretic losses in trained subjects are smaller; yet all of the athletic subjects (10 of 11) either fainted or came near fainting after immersion, while only 3 to 11 untrained did so. All features of fluid and electrolyte function showed lesser changes in the trained subjects. To explain results, these investigators studied urinary secretion of vanillylmandellic acid (VMA) during immersion, a breakdown product of norepinephrine, a main hormone secreted by the sympathetic nervous system (SNS) and adrenals and used to regulate blood pressure. VMA was found to double in nonathletes, and only slightly increase, if at all, in athletes. Such findings can only be explained as a significantly lowered SNS response in athletes. Thus, they provide insight for the first time into possible causes for the poor orthostatic response seen in athletes after immersion, space flight, or bed rest.

The regular presence of an increased plasma volume and decrease in SNS tone may promote a greater dependence in athletic subjects on plasma ADH for blood pressure control. Water immersion, bed rest, and space flight all cause a decrease in circulating blood volume, lowering plasma ADH levels. The decreased orthostatic tolerance after water immersion seems partially compensated in nonathletes by an elevated SNS tone, activated by the blood pressure control system; this compensating control is not used by athletes, who rely more on ADH. Immersion and depression of ADH leave them particularly vulnerable to orthostatic collapse.

Further support for such a possibility and explanation comes from recent tests in our laboratory where ADH levels were measured in individuals able to complete a lower-body negative (LBNP) test. Subjects were divided into nonfainters (high tolerance, N = 8) versus fainters (low tolerance, N = 7). Plasma ADH levels at rest in low tolerance subjects were 0.9 ± 0.3 pg/ml, increasing to 3.1 ± 1.0 pg/ml at peak LBNP; for high tolerance subjects respective levels were $1.5 \pm .05$ pg/ml and 9.3 ± 2.2 pg/ml. Thus, a threefold greater increase in plasma ADH levels at peak LBNP stress was present in the high tolerance versus low tolerance individuals.

Finally, Stegemann, Meier, Skipka, Hartlieb, Hemmer, and Tibes (1975), during 4 to 6 hours of water immersion, demonstrated that severe intermittent swimming (3 minutes each hour) in both trained and untrained subjects could avert the expected urine loss caused by immersion. These changes may help explain one of the great mysteries of space flight. To date there has been little to no diuresis, despite the large headward fluid shifts. This lack may be caused by heavy in-flight exercise and may explain the benefits felt by astronauts and cosmonauts participating in such exercise programs.

SUMMARY

Human physiology is extremely adaptive to its environment. In weightlessness, the human body rapidly adapts to new demands. But major problems occur when the space flight participant returns to earth gravity. Orthostatic intolerance occurs indicating cardiovascular deconditioning, and there is a loss of heart size, bone, and muscle mass. It takes days or weeks to return to normal.

The cosmonaut Valery Ryumin is of particular interest in this regard since he has spent a longer period in space than any human (175 days followed by 185 days with a recovery interval of 8.5 months). Immediately after landing from the 185-day flight, Ryumin, as well as his companion, was described as being nearly incapable of independent movement and suffered orthostatic instability and presyncopal signs when standing. They also showed ECG changes which lasted for 5 to 6 days and occurred despite dietary measures, medication, and in-flight exercise. Similar overall findings were present after the recent 237-day flight.

With regard to space flight, technology now permits development of space stations where humans will spend very long periods in weightlessness. Human welfare must continue to be a primary consideration in all space flight decisions, and this requires continued research to assess the very long-term effects of weightlessness, inactivity, and isolation. Once this information becomes available, there is no reason to believe that humans cannot live and conduct meaningful work in space for several years at a time, should they so desire. In fact, with continuous use and expansion of space station activities, many individuals may not wish to return to earth after these experiences. After 3- to 6-month sojourns in space, some individuals may wish to stay on board provided untoward effects have not become manifest or cannot be detected. In such cases perhaps permanent adaptations may take place. Legs, a key evolutionary development, would not be needed in space. Headward fluid shifts could stimulate greater growth and development of the upper half of the body. Greater reliance on computer interfaces and automated control could stimulate new ways of thinking and means of communications. Regardless of the areas affected, prolonged space flight offers opportunities for humankind to learn more about itself and provide a fertile environment for continued beneficial technological development.

REFERENCES

CONVERTINO, V.A., Sandler, H., Webb, P., & Annis, J.F. (1982). Induced venous pooling and cardiorespiratory responses to exercise after bed rest. *Journal of Applied Physiology,* **52**, 1343-1348.

CONVERTINO, V.A., Benjamin, B.A., Keil, L.C., Savin, W.M., Gordon, E., Haskell, W.L., Schroeder, J.S., & Sandler, H. (1983). Role of cardiac volume receptors in the control of antidiuretic hormone (ADH) release in man. *The Physiologist,* **26**(4), A-60.

DEBUSK, R.F., Convertino, V.A., Hung, J., & Goldwater, D. (1983). Exercise conditioning in middle-aged men after 10 days of bed rest. *Circulation,* **68**, 245-250.

GAZENKO, O.G., Genin, A.M., & Yegorov, A.D. (1981). Summary of medical investigations in the USSR manned space missions. *Acta Astronautica*, **8**, 907-917.

GILMORE, J.P. (1983). Neural control of extracellular volume in the human and non-human primate. In J.T. Shepherd & F.M. Abboud (Eds.), *Handbook of physiology: The cardiovascular system*. Bethesda, MD: American Physiological Society.

KLEIN, K.E., Wegmann, H.A., & Kuklinski, P. (1977). Athletic endurance training—Advantage for space flight? The significance of physical fitness for selection and training of Spacelab crews. *Aviation, Space, and Environmental Medicine*, **48**(3), 215-222.

NICOGOSSIAN, A.E., & Parker, J.F., Jr. (Eds.) (1982). *NASA SP-447, Space physiology and medicine*. Washington, DC: National Aeronautics and Space Administration.

SANDLER, H. (1980). Effects of bedrest and weightlessness on the heart. In G.H. Bourne (Ed.). *Hearts and heart-like organs*. New York: Academic Press.

SKIPKA, W., & Schramm, U. (1982). A critical evaluation of the employment of water immersion techniques in investigations related to physiological reactions during space flight. In *Zero-G simulation for ground-based studies in human physiology, with emphasis on the cardiovascular and body fluid systems*. Paris: European Space Agency (ESA) SP-180.

STEGEMANN, J., Meier, U., Skipka, W., Hartlieb, W., Hemmer, B., & Tibes, U. (1975). Effects of a multi-hour immersion with intermittent exercise on urinary excretion and tilt table tolerance in athletes and nonathletes. *Aviation, Space, and Environmental Medicine*, **46**, 26-29.

THORTON, W. (1981). Rationale for exercise in spaceflight. In *NASA Conference Proceedings on spaceflight and deconditioning and physical fitness*. National Aeronautics and Space Administration Contract NASW 3469.

PRESIDENTS
American Academy of Physical Education

*	1926-30	Clark W. Hetherington
*	1930-38	Robert Tait McKenzie
*	1938-39	Robert Tait McKenzie
		Mabel Lee
*	1939-41	John Brown, Jr.
	1941-43	Mabel Lee
*	1943-45	Arthur H. Steinhaus
*	1945-47	Jay B. Nash
*	1947-49	Charles H. McCloy
*	1949-50	Frederick W. Cozens
*	1950-51	Rosalind Cassidy
	1951-52	Seward C. Staley
*	1952-53	David K. Brace
	1953-54	Neils P. Neilson
	1954-55	Elmer D. Mitchell
	1955-56	Anna S. Espenschade
*	1956-57	Harry A. Scott
*	1957-58	Charles C. Cowell
*	1958-59	Delbert Oberteuffer
	1959-60	Helen Manley
	1960-61	Thomas E. McDonough, Sr.
	1961-62	M. Gladys Scott
	1962-63	Fred V. Hein
	1963-64	Carl L. Nordly
*	1964-65	Eleanor Metheny
	1965-66	Leonard A. Larson
*	1966-67	Arthur A. Esslinger
	1967-68	Margaret G. Fox
	1968-69	Laura J. Huelster
	1969-70	H. Harrison Clarke
	1970-71	Ruth M. Wilson
	1971-72	Ben W. Miller
	1972-73	Raymond A. Weiss
	1973-74	Ann E. Jewett
	1974-75	King J. McCristal
*	1975-76	Leona Holbrook
	1976-77	Marvin H. Eyler
	1977-78	Louis E. Alley
	1978-79	Marguerite A. Clifton
	1979-80	Harold M. Barrow
	1980-81	Aileene S. Lockhart
	1981-82	Earle F. Zeigler
	1982-83	Edward J. Shea
	1983-84	Henry J. Montoye (current)
	1984-85	David H. Clarke (elect)

* deceased

Volume 17

Exercise and Health

Edited by Helen M. Eckert, PhD, and Henry J. Montoye, PhD

Each of the 12 papers in this volume focuses on the relationship of exercise to health. With contributions by leading scholars in the field, this timely book is an excellent reference or text for all professionals and students concerned with exercise and well-being.

Contents

1984 • Paper • 160 pp • ISBN 0-931250-56-0 • Item BECK0056
$12.00—US & Canada • $14.50—Foreign

Human Kinetics Publishers, Inc.
Box 5076, Champaign, IL 61820